MAPPING POVERTY THROUGH DATA INTEGRATION AND ARTIFICIAL INTELLIGENCE

A Special Supplement of the Key Indicators for Asia and the Pacific 2020

SEPTEMBER 2020

ASIAN DEVELOPMENT BANK

ADB

Notes:
In this publication, "$" refers to United States dollars, unless otherwise stated.
ADB recognizes "China" as the People's Republic of China.

Cover design by Rhommell Rico.

Contents

Tables, Figures, and Boxes

Foreword

Can nontraditional data sources, such as satellite imagery, serve as a useful supplementary data source in measuring the Sustainable Development Goals (SDGs)?

Economies worldwide are racing to meet the SDGs by 2030. Pledging to leave no one behind, and to first assist those most in need, the 17 SDGs are monitored through a global framework consisting of hundreds of targets and indicators. The majority of these indicators are compiled by national statistical systems through representative surveys, censuses, and administrative records. For instance, the indicators for SDG 1: Eradication of Poverty conventionally come from surveys on household income and expenditure, or on living standards. Often, such surveys have sample sizes that are large enough to provide nationally representative estimates. These sample sizes generally also provide estimates that fall within tolerable levels of reliability when further disaggregating poverty estimates by significant or established intranational domains, e.g., by states, provinces, or regions. However, survey sample sizes are typically not large enough to provide reliable estimates at more granular levels, such as municipalities and villages, and therefore may not be able to assist policymakers in efficiently targeting population segments that have the greatest need for poverty reduction programs.

Increasing survey sample sizes to produce reliable estimates at granular levels is the ideal option, but it is often not practical. Achieving such increases requires significant additional resources, which are not readily available to national statistics offices (NSOs) or the organizations that conduct national surveys. As an alternative, some countries adopt small area estimation methods, whereby survey data are complemented with auxiliary data from census or administrative records. These auxiliary data sources are very useful because they facilitate further disaggregation of poverty statistics to provide reliable estimates at more granular levels than those for which surveys might be originally designed. However, since census and administrative data are frequently not available or readily accessible, there are studies that explore the use of alternative sources of auxiliary data because such data are not prone to sampling errors.

In 2017, the Asian Development Bank (ADB) designed a knowledge initiative called Data for Development, which aims to strengthen the capacity of NSOs in the Asia and Pacific region to meet the increasing data demands for effective policymaking and for monitoring development goals and targets. One component of the initiative focuses on subnational disaggregation of SDG indicators, particularly poverty statistics. This component draws inspiration from studies that use satellite imagery, geospatial data, and powerful machine-learning algorithms to complement traditional data sources and conventional survey methods. This approach can be used to estimate the magnitude of poverty in specific areas in the world, and the resulting data can aid governments and development organizations in distributing funds more efficiently as well as helping policymakers design more effective and targeted poverty reduction strategies. Statisticians from ADB's Statistics and Data Innovation Unit within the Economic Research and Regional Cooperation Department worked with the Philippine Statistics Authority, the National Statistical Office of Thailand, and the World Data Lab to examine the feasibility of poverty mapping using satellite imagery and associated geospatial data.

This supplement to *Key Indicators for Asia and the Pacific 2020* documents the initial results of the feasibility study, which aimed to explore alternative data collection channels by combining traditional methods with innovative sources that might enhance the granularity, cost effectiveness, and compilation of high-quality poverty statistics. The publication team was led by Arturo Martinez, Jr, under the over all direction of Elaine Tan. Arturo Martinez, Jr., Mildred Addawe, Joseph Albert Niño Bulan, Ron Lester Durante, Katharina Fenz, Martin Hoffer, Marymell Martillan, Thomas Mitterling, and Tomas Sako wrote the report. Wanpen Poonwong, Wichai Pathipthip, Oarawan Sutthangkul, Hataichanok Chinauparwat, Budsara Sangaroon, Saowaluck Inbumrung, Sanonoi Buracharoen, Thitiwat Kaew-Amdee, Bunpot Teemuangsong, and Saratrai Watcharaporn of the National Statistical Office of Thailand, along with Claire Dennis Mapa, Rosalinda Bautista, Candido Astrologo, Jr., Minerva Eloisa Esquivias, Wilma Guillen, Divina Gracia Del Prado, Severa de Costo, Benjamin Navarro, Bernadette Balamban, Justine Angelo Bantang, Patricia Anne San Buenaventura, Anna Jean Pascasio, Driesch Cortel, and Mechelle Viernes of the Philippine Statistics Authority, and ADB consultants Katrina Miradora, Jan Arvin Lapuz, Zita Albacea, Jose Ramon Albert, Erniel Barrios, Joseph Ryan Lansangan, Nattapong Puttanapong, and Bastian Zaini, all contributed to works that were used as inputs and references for this report. Kristofer Hamel and ADB's Kaushal Joshi provided insightful feedback that helped refine the findings of the study, while participants at the Big Data Analytics workshop contributed valuable comments and feedback. François Fonteneau of the Partnership in Statistics for Development in the 21st Century, Arman Bidarbakht-Nia and Sharita Serrao of the United Nations Economic and Social Commission for Asia and the Pacific, and Haoyi Chen and Yongyi Min of the United Nations Statistics Division, Daniel Clarke, Jonggun Lee, and Rana Hasan provided valuable insights during the conceptualization of the technical assistance project. Criselda De Dios and Iva Sebastian, with the assistance of Ma. Roselia Babalo, Oth Marulou Gagni, Aileen Gatson, and Rose Anne Dumayas provided operational support through the course of the project. The cover of this supplement was designed by Rhommell Rico. Cai Ordinario provided editing services, ensuring coherence and consistency. Manuscript editing was performed by Paul Dent, while the publication's layout, page design, and typesetting were carried out by Rhommell Rico.

We hope this publication will be useful for NSOs across Asia and the Pacific, helping them to consider innovative data sources as means of delivering high-quality, granular, and cost-effective data for SDG monitoring and poverty reduction programs.

Yasuyuki Sawada
Chief Economist and Director General
Economic Research and Regional Cooperation Department
Asian Development Bank

Highlights

- **Granular statistics on poverty can empower public policymakers and enable them to deliver improved programs and services for the poor and most vulnerable segments of society.** However, achieving granularity typically requires increasing the sample sizes of surveys on household income and expenditure or living standards, an option that is not always feasible for national statistics offices (NSOs) or the organizations that conduct these surveys.

- **The 2030 Sustainable Development Agenda recommends that development indicators, including poverty statistics, be disaggregated by location, gender, age, income, and other relevant dimensions.** These informational requirements further magnify the need for granular statistics, making data collection more challenging than ever for national statistics systems, especially those operating within developing countries and/or on limited resources.

- **Innovations in digital technology present exciting opportunities to embrace a new paradigm of sourcing data for development purposes.** In particular, applications to use data from digital transactions, telecommunications records, social media, and remote sensing are expanding. Such data can deliver better understanding of development issues and provide policymakers with a continuous flow of timely and granular information to make decisions.

- **It is important to note that innovative sources of data are not perfect substitutes for the traditional data sources on which many official statistics are based.** Whereas compilation of official statistics is based on scientifically rigorous guidelines vetted by experts to ensure representativeness, accuracy, and reliability, concerns about potential bias accompanying the use of new data sources abound.

- **Data integration is an effective way to make the most of conventional and innovative sources of data.** In compiling poverty statistics, for instance, advances in machine-learning algorithms have propelled the field of image analysis forward and created opportunities to blend satellite imagery with conventional sources of poverty data. Such integration of complementary data can help achieve the level of granularity that sheds light on a country's true spatial distribution of socioeconomic disadvantage.

- **Exploring the feasibility of a poverty estimation method that incorporates satellite imagery does not aim to replace conventional methods.** Rather, it sets out to address some of the limitations associated with traditional poverty estimation techniques. The results derived from new techniques could also be used to validate findings produced using traditional methodologies, which may serve as a means of building trust in poverty statistics compiled by NSOs.

- **Recognizing the important role that NSOs play in compiling granular poverty statistics, ADB implemented a knowledge initiative within two pilot economies: the Philippines and Thailand.** The initiative aims to strengthen the capacity of NSOs to meet data demands for effective poverty monitoring, by complementing traditional data sources with nontraditional data, particularly information extracted from satellite imagery through computer vision techniques.

- **The Philippines and Thailand were strategically chosen for the research study because both countries had existing initiatives to combine household survey data with census data to produce more granular yet**

reliable estimates of poverty. The initiatives in both countries provided sufficient data on which computer vision algorithms could be trained. In addition, the Philippines and Thailand have slightly different poverty profiles, allowing for an examination of how poverty distribution might affect granular poverty estimation that incorporates data from satellite imagery.

- **The results of applying the integrated study methodology on specific datasets from the Philippines and Thailand are encouraging.** Even using publicly accessible satellite imagery, in which the resolutions are not as fine as those in commercially sourced images, the study produced predictions that aligned with the government-published poverty estimates.

- **The study methodology met the primary objective of providing poverty estimates that are more granular than those currently being compiled by the NSOs in the Philippines and Thailand.** Better still, further gains in the granularity of statistics potentially can be made if higher resolution imagery is used in future studies.

- **For the purposes of small-scale poverty studies using nontraditional data, NSOs can streamline their resources and avoid substantial upfront costs by capitalizing on publicly accessible satellite imagery, affordable cloud services, and computational tools.** However, data-sourcing activities on a larger and more meaningful scale might require NSOs to make significant investments in higher resolution imagery, faster local computation equipment, and the vast volumes of internet bandwidth required to manage high volumes of data. It is also important for NSOs to expand their investments in human capital, such as appropriately skilled data scientists, to collect, process, and analyze geospatial and other nontraditional data, and to integrate new data collection methodologies into their work programs.

- **As they strive to meet the data demands of monitoring the Sustainable Development Agenda and ensuring evidence-based policymaking, NSOs should not operate in isolation.** The generation of development statistics using nontraditional data sources is a complex ecosystem that informs and impacts multiple stakeholders, including governments, private enterprises, academic and financial institutions, technology companies, and the general public. Forging partnerships and cooperation between these stakeholders has the potential to deliver access to large volumes of innovative data, so long as optimal confidentiality frameworks are maintained. Furthermore, ongoing engagement between data stakeholders and policymakers can help ensure that the statistics being compiled by NSOs are used to enhance society and improve living standards, particularly for the poor and disadvantaged.

Introduction

In 2015, a few months before global leaders met at United Nations Headquarters in New York to launch the Sustainable Development Goals (SDGs)—renewing the world's commitment to eradicate all forms of poverty, narrow the gap between rich and poor, and promote long-term development—the story of a young Filipino boy graced various social media platforms in the Philippines.

In the photograph that went viral on the internet, 9-year-old Daniel Cabrera was seen studying on the sidewalk of a busy street corner, by the lights of a popular fast food restaurant. The powerful image, which depicted the boy's commitment to his studies despite his socioeconomic circumstances, attracted the attention of many thousands of people who, in turn, helped Daniel and his family to make ends meet. Through the exposure and support achieved via the internet, Daniel later received a scholarship (Yam 2015) and has since graduated from grade school (Tizon 2019), while his mother has been able to find steady and stable employment.

Although Daniel's story is heartwarming, it is not unique. One can easily find tales of hope and resilience on the internet, where netizens collectively help people overcome social and economic challenges after their stories are shared on the web. Such stories create narratives that evoke emotions, sway opinions, justify certain courses of action, or inspire further exploration: they serve as catalysts for development momentum.

From cave paintings and other ancient forms of storytelling through to the invention of the printing press, the telephone, and the television, technological advances in communication have made it possible for humans to recount historical events, learn from the lessons of the past, and inspire collective action. The advent of the internet paved the way for the birth of social media, which is changing the way human stories are shared and information is relayed, both within small local communities and around the world.

However, personal stories and inspiring anecdotes alone will not have sufficient impact to improve the lives of the many millions of people who have significant income challenges and face the stresses of poverty each and every day. Stories supported by reliable data provide a far more compelling narrative and can yield greater development impact.

One example where data and statistics have been used to make a difference in improving lives and livelihoods is the case of Siayan, a municipality in the province of Zamboanga del Norte in the southern part of the Philippines.

Prior to the early 2000s, reliable data on poverty in specific municipalities of the Philippines were not available because the survey used to estimate poverty statistics was designed to provide estimates at higher geographic levels. However, thanks to the efforts of statisticians from the Philippine Statistics Authority (PSA)[1] in collaboration with the country's development partners, poverty data at the municipality level became available. Based on these statistics, Siayan was found to be among the poorest municipalities in the Philippines. In fact, with a poverty incidence of 97.5%, it was listed as the poorest municipality in the country in 2003 (PSA 2009).

The availability of granular statistics shed light on the magnitude of poverty in Siayan, highlighting the number of people at risk of socioeconomic exclusion. The Government of the Philippines and other development institutions worked together to turn this situation around and improve the lives of Siayanons. As a result, when the PSA released its municipality-level poverty estimates for 2015, the poverty incidence in Siayan was estimated at 68.4%. For 2 consecutive survey years, Siayan has not been listed among the 10 poorest municipalities in the Philippines.

---

[1] These efforts were initiated by the former National Statistical Coordination Board, which is now part of the Philippine Statistics Authority.

Statisticians can take motivation and inspiration from Siayan's accomplishments as they underline the importance of producing quality data for development. Statistical outcomes are critical inputs to evidence-based policymaking because they contribute so greatly to designing, monitoring, and evaluating development strategies aimed at achieving a country or region's social, economic, and environmental priorities. Development practitioners can use data as leverage to speak on behalf of people who may be left behind by inequitable economic progress. Data that are timely and reliable should be at the core of policy formulation on crucial development issues. This is even more vital as the world approaches the deadline of achieving the 2030 Sustainable Development Agenda.

Amid global accomplishment on poverty reduction, which is the first and primary SDG, much effort is needed to elevate more people above the poverty line. The latest global poverty statistics compiled by the World Bank suggest that 736.7 million people are still living on less than $1.90 a day. Worryingly, the recent pandemic brought by the novel coronavirus might have pushed even more people into poverty (Park et al. 2020; Sumner et al. 2020). That represents millions of stories like Daniel Cabrera's, waiting to be told in order to inspire collective action.

Unfortunately, tracking progress on poverty reduction is not an easy task. Conventionally, poverty statistics are compiled by conducting a household income or expenditure survey (HIES) or a living standards survey (LSS). Scaling up these efforts in traditional, household-based data collection can be costly for national statistics offices (NSOs), particularly those in developing countries. Estimates from the Sustainable Development Solutions Network (2015) suggest that the cost of conducting a HIES is approximately $1.7 million. Not surprisingly, many countries cannot conduct these types of surveys on a regular basis. In Asia and the Pacific, more than a dozen countries collect data via a HIES or LSS less frequently than every 5 years.

Nevertheless, just as social media and other communications technologies are being leveraged to efficiently disseminate data stories to a wide audience, there is also enormous potential for NSOs and other producers of development statistics to take advantage of innovative and emerging data sources.

The generation of poverty statistics is an area in which there are exciting opportunities to blend traditional data sources and administrative records with information extracted from satellite imagery (Castelan et al. 2019). Given the high cost of conducting detailed expenditure or income surveys, increasing a survey's sample size to reflect all geographic areas and different population groupings may not be a practical option. Moreover, the relevance and timeliness of reliable poverty statistics require that such surveys be conducted every two or three years. Adding nontraditional and innovative data sources into the mix can potentially address the restrictions that conventional data sources used for poverty estimation may have on granularity and timeliness.

Satellite imagery is an excellent example of an innovative data source that falls outside the traditional paradigm of reference points used by NSOs to compile official poverty statistics. While NSOs typically only conduct surveys and censuses to collect data, case studies show that geospatial data and other information extracted from satellite imagery, when used to complement traditionally sourced data, can provide richer insights on various development topics. In fact, just 1 year after the United Nations Statistical Commission established the Inter-Agency and Expert Group on SDG Indicators (IAEG-SDGs) in 2015, the Working Group on Geospatial Information was created to provide guidance to the IAEG-SDGs on the role of NSOs in considering geospatial data and Earth observations. This move was intended as a means to contribute to, and validate, datasets as part of official statistics for SDG indicators (IAEG-SDGs 2016).

In 2017, recognizing the importance of reliable data in meeting the SDGs as well as the central role NSOs can play as primary producers of official statistics, ADB designed a knowledge initiative called Data for Development. The initiative aims to strengthen the capacity of NSOs across Asia and Pacific to meet the increasing data demands for policymaking and monitoring of development goals and targets. One component of the initiative focuses on subnational disaggregation of SDG indicators, particularly poverty statistics. This component draws on findings from recently concluded and ongoing studies that use satellite imagery, geospatial data, and powerful machine-learning algorithms in tandem with traditional data sources and conventional methods of determining poverty. By doing so, these studies are able to estimate poverty levels in particular areas in the world, providing governments and development organizations with reliable and specific information on which to base the efficient distribution of funds and the formulation of effective and targeted policies.

Statisticians from ADB's Statistics and Data Innovation Unit worked with the PSA, the National Statistical Office of Thailand, and the World Data Lab to examine the feasibility of poverty mapping using satellite imagery and associated geospatial data. Both the Philippines and Thailand have existing initiatives to combine household survey data with census data to produce more granular yet reliable estimates of poverty, and these initiatives provide sufficient data on which machine-learning algorithms can be trained. The two countries, although both considered to be middle-income countries, have slightly different poverty profiles and poverty estimation methodology, with Thailand showing significantly lower poverty rates than the Philippines. This allows for an examination of how poverty distribution affects the feasibility of the alternative poverty estimation method discussed in this report.

This supplement outlines the initial results of the feasibility study conducted via the collaboration between ADB, the NSOs of the Philippines and Thailand, and the World Data Lab. The objective of the study is to explore alternative data collection strategies by combining traditional survey methods with innovative data sources to enhance the granularity, cost effectiveness, and quality of poverty statistics.[2] Such data collection strategies could be immensely useful for countries that rely solely on resource-intensive surveys to compile poverty statistics. In addition to discussing the methodology and preliminary findings of the feasibility study, the supplement delivers some key considerations for the sustainable integration of innovative data sources, particularly satellite imagery, into the work programs of NSOs in developing countries.

Estimating Poverty Using Conventional Data Sources

By compiling poverty statistics, data can be made to speak on behalf of people who are experiencing severe socioeconomic disadvantage, making them visible to the policymakers who set the development agenda. This entails having data to indicate who the poor are, where they live, how many are poor, and why they are poor. The availability of geographically disaggregated poverty statistics helps answer some of these questions and allows policymakers to see a clearer and more detailed profile of the poor. Of course, the more granular the level of poverty statistics, the more accurately this profile analysis can be done.

When the poor are identified by using granular data as evidence for policymaking, more efficient and effective strategies and programs on poverty reduction

---

[2] There are parallel initiatives that use satellite imagery for poverty mapping in the countries covered by this study. For example, an initiative called Thinking Machines uses a similar satellite-image-based method to predict wealth in the Philippines (Tingzon et al. 2019). However, since their input data are solely based on surveys (whereas the study for this supplement uses small area poverty estimates) when training machine-learning algorithms, the poverty estimates used during algorithm-training in the supplement study are less prone to large sampling error. Similarly, studies in Thailand focus on correlating poverty with intensity of night lights (Dorji 2019).

can be formulated. Initiatives such as social protection programs, including cash transfers and employment facilitation, can better aim to improve the specific plight of the poor and disadvantaged. Once such initiatives are in place, the availability of granular poverty data can also be used for program monitoring and evaluation, revealing the true impact of programs such as tax reforms, cash transfers, and employment programs for the poor.

In many developing countries of Asia and the Pacific, official poverty numbers are estimated and made available at national, regional, provincial, or other highly aggregated levels. However, the NSOs of some countries, in collaboration with development partners, strive to further disaggregate poverty statistics.

Statisticians spend time and resources to estimate poverty objectively and accurately. The objective measurement of poverty starts with the identification of the welfare metric, which serves as basis for assessing whether or not a person or household is poor. Income and expenditure are two of the commonly used metrics for poverty measurement, but there are advantages and disadvantages in using these metrics.

After identifying the welfare metric, the next step is to determine the poverty line. When measuring absolute poverty—the severe deprivation of basic human needs such as food, safe drinking water, sanitation facilities, health, shelter, education, and information (UN 1995)—many countries tend to adopt an approach that measures the cost of basic needs. This approach identifies a food basket that achieves the minimum nutritional requirements set by the World Health Organization and the Food and Agriculture Organization of the United Nations. The minimum nutritional requirements vary across countries due to the levels of activity and average weights of each population.[3] The World Bank, which measures poverty

across countries using a comparable standard, has set an absolute international poverty line based on the 2011 purchasing power parity (PPP) of $1.90 per day. In contrast, more developed countries set their poverty lines based on relative standards. The relative poverty line of each country is usually expressed as a function of the median income level of a family or individual (UN 2005).

Another common practice in poverty estimation is to allow for the equivalence scale and make adjustments accordingly. The equivalence scale simply means that families or households with the same levels of income or expenditure are not necessarily equally rich or equally poor. The economic status of a family or household also depends on household size and/or its composition, such as the number of working-age adults, children, and elderly members. In many cases, income or expenditure is simply divided by the household size, and the resulting per capita equivalent is used to assess whether the household sits above or below a predetermined poverty line. Poverty data can also be estimated based on the age of household members. NSOs often assign index weights according to the age of household members.

Due to the wide array of information needed to estimate poverty, household income and expenditure surveys or living standard surveys are the collection vehicle of choice to gather appropriate data. As with other household surveys, the required granularity for reliable poverty estimates must be reflected by an appropriate survey sample size. This often calls for difficult policy and administrative decisions because NSOs generally need to strike a balance between meeting the data needs of policymakers and assigning the resources available to them.

An alternative way of generating granular poverty statistics, while keeping survey costs at manageable

---

[3]   The Philippines and Thailand, countries that are featured in this study, employ slightly different methodologies to establish minimum nutritional requirements. For instance, the reported minimum caloric threshold in the Philippines is 2,000 calories per person per day (PSA 2007), without adjustment for age, gender, and location. Meanwhile, the minimum caloric threshold in Thailand is differentiated by age and gender, and is set at 2,100 calories for men and 1,750 calories for women aged 31 to 50 (Haughton and Khandker 2009).

levels, is small area estimation (SAE). When using SAE, survey data are complemented by other conventional data sources, such as census or administrative records, which provide auxiliary information that can contribute to more specific poverty estimates (ADB 2020).

The World Bank's poverty mapping methodology—also known as the Elbers, Lanjouw, and Lanjouw (ELL) technique (2003)—is one of the most popular applications of SAE in more than 70 countries (WB 2007). In principle, poverty mapping integrates income or expenditure data from national household surveys with auxiliary data from population censuses (ideally collected in the same year). The poverty mapping methodology first employs survey data to build a welfare model or an income or expenditure model. This is then applied to census data to yield predicted values of expenditure or income for each household. These predicted values are used to estimate poverty and inequality estimates at the small area level (Das and Chambers 2015). Table 1 shows a list of some countries in Asia and the Pacific that employ the ELL technique.

In addition to providing poverty and inequality maps, the technique has been used to produce nutritional data on stunting and wasting, as well as health and disease maps, in a number of developing countries (Van der Weide 2017).

There are, however, several technical issues associated with conventional SAE methods. For instance, a limitation of the ELL technique arises when estimates are to be compiled for years that fall between censuses. Comparability of variables can result in statistical errors when the household survey and the census do not have the same reference year. To rectify such errors, SAE variables can be examined to identify which ones have characteristics that do not vary over time and therefore can be included in the SAE model (ADB 2020). Of course, imposing this criterion limits the number of covariates that can be included in the analysis and the adequacy of the model is affected as a result.

Using Big Data to Enhance Development Statistics

The use of methods such as SAE highlights the benefits of integrating multiple data sources to derive poverty statistics. However, as noted, technical issues may arise even after combining multiple conventional data sources such as survey, census, and administrative data. It is therefore useful to look at nonconventional data sources as well.

Studies suggest that big data—particularly in the form of geospatial data and mobile phone data—have great potential in enhancing the compilation of a wide range of development statistics (Eagle et al. 2010; Data2X 2017). For example, in terms of cost, it is far less expensive to access mobile phone data than to conduct a national household survey—assuming private telecommunications companies are willing to share

Table 1: Select Countries in Asia and the Pacific that Use the World Bank's Poverty Mapping Methodology	
Country	Level of Disaggregation of Poverty Estimates
Afghanistan	district, nahia
Armenia	district
Azerbaijan	rayon (district)
Bangladesh	upazila (subdistrict)
Bhutan	subdistrict
Cambodia	commune
Fiji	tikina (district)
Georgia	municipality
India	district
Indonesia	village
Lao People's Democratic Republic	district
Mongolia	soum (district)
Nepal	village
Pakistan	district
Papua New Guinea	local level government area
Philippines	city, municipality
Sri Lanka	district
Thailand	subdistrict
Viet Nam	district

Note: The table is not a full and comprehensive list of countries in Asia and the Pacific that use the World Bank's poverty mapping methodology.
Sources: Asian Development Bank. 2016. *Key Indicators for Asia and the Pacific 2016*. Manila; and compilation by the study team using data from international development organizations.

such data. With respect to timeliness, since telephone logs and satellite images are generally collected every day, mobile phone and geospatial data can be accessed almost in real time (Pizatella-Haswell 2018).

There is a need to understand how innovative data sources can be used to enhance the compilation of statistics. If having more granular statistics is the main objective, extending the SAE framework can be one of the many options available (Box 1). The specific technique will be dictated by the survey objective, the type of statistics for which the compilation process needs to be enhanced, and the type of data available.

Predicting Poverty Using Geospatial Data

Building on the potential to incorporate nontraditional data into conventional poverty estimation methods is the notion of using geospatial data, particularly from satellite imagery, for such purposes. Although poverty estimation can also benefit from using mobile phone records (Blumenstock et al. 2015) and other sources of big data, the accessibility of satellite imagery can be a persuasive factor in encouraging more NSOs to consider using this particular data source in compiling

---

Box 1: Integration of Big Data into a Small Area Estimation Framework

Marchetti et al. (2015) explain three possible approaches to integrating big data into a small area estimation (SAE) framework: (i) generate granular indicators from big data and correlate them with SAE-derived indicators, (ii) generate covariates from big data sources and include them as auxiliary variables in SAE models, and (iii) employ survey data to examine and eliminate the self-selection bias of big data values.

In the first approach, granular data can be extracted from big data sources. While it is deemed more efficient and timely to collect and process big data than conventional data, some types of big data may be contaminated with self-selection bias. To check for such bias, the indicators gathered from big data must be compared with the indicators derived from the SAE technique. If the data is comparable at the small area level, it can be assumed that the big data source can potentially provide reliable benchmark information. However, if the two data sets are not comparable, further studies must be conducted to examine the variable of interest at the small area level.

The second approach entails generating new covariates from big data sources and employing them as auxiliary variables in statistical modeling. SAE is essentially about integrating survey data with auxiliary data to improve the granularity of estimates. Auxiliary data are not limited to census, administrative, and other survey data sources: they can also be sourced from social media, global positioning systems, or remotely sensed images, which can provide an indication of the socioeconomic situation at the small area level. However, there are advantages and disadvantages in using big data covariates. While big data can offer rich information on various socioeconomic and demographic outcomes, they may require more complex SAE techniques to solve potential sampling and nonsampling errors associated with these data.

In the last approach, the distribution of values of survey data and big data is evaluated to ensure consistency and reliability. In big data, the issue of representativeness of the data must be considered if the objective is to estimate the marginalized segments of the population. Any serious self-selection bias associated with big data can render these estimates problematic. These constraints can be addressed by examining the common variables between survey data and big data, measuring the differences between variables and using these differences to estimate weights to reduce the self-selection bias. Other correlated variables can be explored if there are no common variables between the survey data and the big data.

Reference
S. Marchetti, et al. 2015. Small Area Model-Based Estimators Using Big Data Sources. *Journal of Official Statistics*, 31(2): 263-281.

poverty statistics. It is relatively straightforward to scale up initiatives using data derived from satellite imagery.

Box 2 provides a snapshot of different ways that geospatial data can be used to predict poverty. Among these are recent poverty prediction methodologies, such as that of Jean et al. (2016), which are rapidly

Box 2: Two Broad Methods of Predicting Poverty Using Geospatial Data

In the academic literature on using nontraditional data sources to estimate poverty, there are essentially two broad methods discussed.

The first broad method entails developing a structural model for predicting poverty by using covariates from geospatial data and other information that can be derived from satellite imagery. In a study conducted by the World Bank, models based on high resolution spatial imagery variables—such as building density and number, shadow area, car counts, road density, farmland type, roof material, and vegetation index, among others—were used. These models were developed to explain variations in poverty levels between villages in developing countries such as Sri Lanka. The results showed strong correlation between the spatial imagery variables and predicted poverty, where 40% to 60% of the predicted variations in village-level poverty could be explained by geospatial data from the satellite imagery (Engstrom, Hersch, and Newhouse 2016). A similar methodological framework was used in the Tuscany region of Italy, where big data on mobility, e.g., the movement of private vehicles, were tracked with a global positioning system device and used as covariates in an area-level model. This enabled researchers to estimate actual poverty head counts and mean household incomes (calculated according to the number of equivalent adults in each household) in local labor systems (Marchetti et al. 2015).

While these studies have structural models through which covariates aligned with poverty can be identified to allow econometric interpretation, the second broad method for predicting poverty is more abstract. It does not have a clear structural model and relies on algorithms based on neural networks and deep machine learning. For instance, researchers in rural India are training a multilayered machine model to predict poverty using information obtained from satellite imagery—roof materials, light sources, and drinking water sources along with other features such as roads, farms, and bodies of water. The model then predicts incomes for the same satellite areas and estimates the poverty level in each area (Pandey et al. 2018). A similar study has applied deep-learning techniques to predict poverty in six cities of North and South America: Boston, Chicago, Houston, Los Angeles, and Philadelphia in the United States; and Santiago in Chile (Piaggesi et al. 2019). Methods falling under the second broad method tend to perform better in prediction-related tasks.

One of the most frequently cited studies that followed the second broad method was conducted by researchers from Stanford University and later published in the journal Science (Jean et al. 2016). The main objective of the study was to estimate the prevalence of poverty by simply examining high resolution satellite imagery. Given that data from satellite images are highly unstructured, attempting to manually examine all features, and to correlate such features with varying levels of poverty, would prove to be difficult. A more efficient approach was to develop a powerful algorithm that automated the process of predicting poverty levels correlating to specific geographic locations.

References

R. Engstrom, J. Hersch, and D.L. Newhouse. 2016. Poverty in HD: What Does High Resolution Satellite Imagery Reveal about Economic Welfare?

N. Jean, et al. 2016. Combining satellite imagery and machine learning to predict poverty. *Science*, 353(6301): 790-794.

S. Marchetti, et al. 2015. Small Area Model-Based Estimators Using Big Data Sources. *Journal of Official Statistics*, 31(2): 263-281.

S. Pandey, et al. 2018. Multi-task deep learning for predicting poverty from satellite images. Thirty Second AAAI Conference on Artificial Intelligence.

S. Piagessi, et al. 2019. Predicting City Poverty Using Satellite Imagery. The IEEE Conference on Computer Vision and Pattern Recognition (CVPR) Workshops. 90-96.

gaining attention among development practitioners. These methodologies capitalize on three fields of artificial intelligence: machine learning, deep learning, and computer vision. These concepts are explained in detail in Appendix 1 and other references (Goodfellow et al. 2016), but are briefly defined here as follows:

> **Machine learning** is a term used to describe algorithms that are designed to automatically learn from data and make responsive decisions, rather than using preprogrammed rules.

> **Deep learning** is attributed to those machine-learning algorithms that follow a logical sequence inspired by how a human brain would make decisions.

> **Computer vision** is an element of machine learning that deals with how computers develop high-level understanding of patterns depicted in digital images.

The images in Figure 1 illustrate what a machine-learning algorithm can do in a task based on computer vision. In this instance, the computer vision is a digital scan of a numeric character, which may have been written down by a researcher in the field. For humans, it is easy to recognize that the first image in Figure 1 shows the character: "7". For a computer, without any vision recognition techniques, the image is just a series of pixel values. To make the image meaningful to a computer, one needs to train the computer to spot "features" and assign them to a particular category. In the second image in Figure 1, the machine-learning algorithm filters horizontal edges, while in the third it filters vertical edges. These simple geometric filters constitute the initial steps or layers of a deep-learning algorithm. Progressively, as the algorithm's learning process deepens, it can eventually filter more complicated features and combination of them in an image. Rather than edges or simple shapes, the more advanced layers of the algorithm should be able to

filter more sophisticated patterns until the algorithm is able to classify them into their appropriate categories. Note that, in deep learning tasks, a priori, these filters usually are unknown to the researcher. The exact make up starts out random, and through the learning process, develops into complex filters.

Figure 1: Illustration of a Computer Vision Task

Source: Computer vision generated by the study team.

To successfully recognize specific features and identify what is featured in an image, an algorithm such as a convolutional neural network (CNN) which is a type of a deep learning algorithm needs volumes and volumes of "labelled" images to train on (e.g., Krizhevsky, et al. 2012). A labelled image is one in which we already know its classification. To achieve standard deep-learning approaches to interpreting imagery, hundreds of thousands or even millions of labelled images are required to successfully train the algorithm (e.g., Krizhevsky, et al. 2012).

In the context of poverty estimation, labelled images at granular levels are limited. Most poverty statistics compiled by NSOs are available at national, regional, or provincial levels. In some countries that use conventional SAE techniques, poverty statistics may also be available at more granular levels, e.g., the district level. Nonetheless, even a country with poverty statistics for 5,000 districts, and therefore 5,000 poverty-labelled images, still may not have sufficient images to train an algorithm to successfully predict poverty (Krizhevsky, et al.)[4].

---

4   In addition to the number of labelled images, the performance of the algorithm also depends on the resolution and quality of the images.

To address this issue, a study conducted by Jean et al. (2016) proposed a transfer learning approach by which, an algorithm is first trained to predict the intensity of night lights as an intermediate step to obtain more granular poverty data. Using data on night lights as a proxy for economic development is arguably valid if it is assumed that places that are brighter at night are generally more economically developed than those places that are less well lit. The advantage of training an algorithm to predict intensity of night lights is that sources of night light data, particularly satellite imagery, are readily accessible and can cost-effectively provide large volumes of labelled images on which to train an algorithm. The result is significantly more granular data than those available through conventional poverty estimates. Without explicitly instructing the computer what to look for, a deep-learning algorithm can soon learn to pick out many features that are easily recognizable to the human eye—such as roads or bridges, buildings, cars, or agricultural land—and can be correlated with the intensity of night lights. Once the algorithm has learned to associate specific features of an image with different levels of intensity of night lights, the knowledge can be transferred to predict poverty (Jean et al. 2016).

In addition to its association with poverty levels, there is some evidence of a close association between the intensity of night lights and economic growth, population growth, and other development indicators (Box 3).

Box 3: Other Development Applications of Night Light Data

There have been many studies that made use of satellite luminosity data as a proxy for other conventional social and economic indicators (Addison and Stewart 2015; Keola et al. 2015). Henderson et al. (2012) used night lights to measure economic growth in several countries. Lo (2001) evaluated the use of night lights as a potential source of population data at the provincial, country, and city levels in the People's Republic of China (PRC). It was found that the operational line scan of the United States Air Force Defense Meteorological Satellite Program (DMSP-OLS) nighttime data produced reasonably accurate estimates of nonagricultural or urban populations at both the county and city levels. Similar analyses to estimate the size of nonagricultural populations were made by Amaral et al. (2006) for the Brazilian Amazon. Likewise, Sutton (1997) found that spatial analysis of the clusters of saturated pixels may be useful to improve maps and datasets of human population distributions in areas of the world where good census data may not be available or do not exist.

Ghosh et. al. (2010) developed statistical models to calibrate the sum of night lights with official measures of economic activity at the subnational level for India, Mexico, the PRC, and the United States, and at the national level for other countries in the world. The study developed unique coefficients that, when applied to night light data, provided estimates of total economic activity and were able to generate spatially disaggregated maps of this activity.

A study by Zhou et. al (2015) found that night light data are capable of providing comprehensive information regarding economic inequality at multiple geographic levels, which is not possible through the use of traditional statistical sources. Yao (2012) constructed a statistical model that established a connection between the intensity of lights in DMSP-OLS images and the combined factors of population and gross domestic product within prefecture-level cities in the PRC.

Further, Akiyama (2012) conducted a study on the use of DMSP-OLS data and the impact of roads on light intensities in Japan. The study demonstrated that the impact of road distribution is strong in urban and suburban areas, while the impact of buildings is strong in rural areas.

(continued on next page)

Box 3: Other Development Applications of Night Light Data   *(continued)*

There are, however, other studies that point to the inaccuracy of DMSP-OLS data in providing good metrics for economic activity of certain regions. Mellander et. al. (2013) found that the link between night lights and economic activity, especially when estimated by wages, is slightly overestimated in large urban areas and underestimated in rural areas.

Chen and Nordhaus (2010, 2011) concluded that satellite luminosity data provide very little added value for countries with high-quality statistical systems. However, such data may be useful for countries with the lowest statistical capacities, particularly for war-torn countries with no recent economic surveys or population censuses. The results also indicated that luminosity data offer more added value when estimating economic density than when attempting to generate time series growth rates.

References

D. Addison, and B. Stewart. 2015. Nighttime Lights Revisited: The Use of Nighttime Lights Data as a Proxy for Economic Variables. World Bank Policy Research Working Paper No. 7496.

Y. Akiyama. 2012. Analysis of Light Intensity Data by the DMSP-OLS Satellite Image Using Existing Spatial Data for Monitoring Human Activity in Japan. ISPRS Annals of the Photogrammetry, Remote Sensing and Spatial Information Sciences.

S. Amaral, et al. 2006. DMSP/OLS night-time light imagery for urban population estimates in the Brazilian Amazon. *International Journal of Remote Sensing.* 25: 855-870.

X. Chen and W.D. Nordhaus, 2010. The Value of Luminosity Data as a Proxy for Economic Statistics. *NBER Working Paper* 16317. Cambridge MA: National Bureau of Economic Research.

_____. 2011. Using Luminosity Data as a Proxy for Economic Statistics. Proceedings of the National Academy of Sciences 108 (21): 8589-8594.

T. Ghosh. et al. 2010. Shedding Light on the Global Distribution of Economic Activity. *The Open Geography Journal* 3: 147-160.

J. Henderson, A. Storeygard, and D. Weil. 2012. Measuring Economic Growth from Outer Space. *American Economic Review*, 102(2), pp. 994-1028.

S. Keola, et al. 2015. Monitoring Economic Development from Outer Space: Using Nighttime Light and Land Cover Data to Measure Economic Growth. *World Development*, 66, pp. 322-334.

C. P. Lo. 2001. Modelling the Population of China Using DMSP Operational Linescan System Nightime Data. *Photogrammetric Engineering & Remote Sensing* 67: 1037-1047.

C. Mellander, et al. 2013. Night-Time Light Data: A Good Proxy Measure for Economic Activity? *Working Paper Series in Economics and Institutions of Innovation* 315, The Royal Institute of Technology, Centre of Excellence for Science and Innovation Studies.

P. Sutton. 1997. Modelling population density with night-time satellite imagery and GIS. *Computers, Environment and Urban Systems.* 21(3/4):227-244.

Yongling Yao, Y. 2012. Correlation of Human Activities with Population and GDP in Chinese Cities - Based on the Data of DMSP-OLS, International Journal of Economics and Management Engineering, 2, pp. 125-128.

Y. Zhou, et al. 2015. Nighttime Light Derived Assessment of Regional Inequality of Socioeconomic Development in China. *Remote Sensing*, 7, pp. 1242-1262. 10.3390/rs70201242.

Using Neural Networks to Develop an Algorithm

Algorithms performing vision-based task are usually based on a neural network, a concept inspired by the human brain. A neural network consists of nodes called neurons and these neurons are connected to each other.

The neural network is divided into three main parts: input layer at the start, hidden layers in the middle, and an output layer (Figure 2). The input layer takes in the raw data. When doing image analysis, the input layer simply corresponds to data from a digital image and each pixel value is stored in a neuron. In the hidden layers, each neuron serves as a filter and is activated each time it detects a specific pattern or feature. The

Figure 2: Illustration of a Neural Network

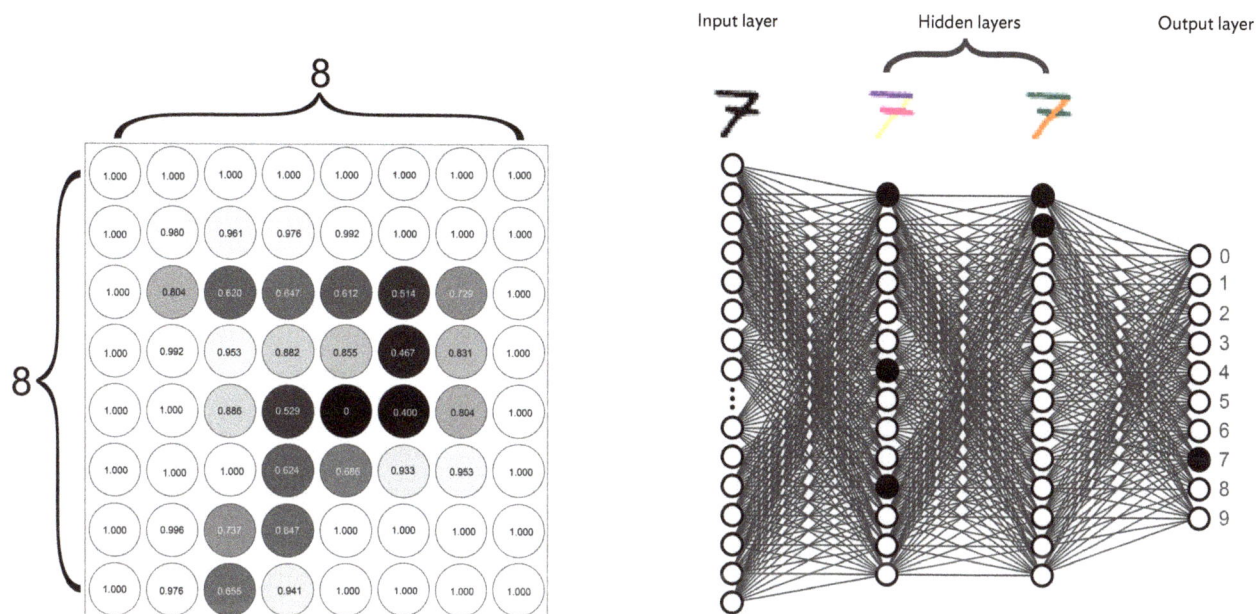

Source: Graphics generated by the study team.

output layer simply identifies the appropriate category to which the image belongs.

Illustrating the inner workings of a neural network can be done using the digitally scanned image of the handwritten numeric character "7" (Figure 1). Suppose there are other images showing different numeric characters and a neural network is to be developed that can identify which of these images represents the number "7". It can be assumed that the digital image is formatted as an 8-pixel x 8-pixel image (the pixels may vary). Hence, the neural network's input layer begins with 64 neurons, corresponding to each of the 8 pixels x 8 pixels.

On the left side of Figure 2, each neuron in the input layer is associated with a number that represents the grayscale value of the corresponding pixel. Grayscale values typically range from zero to 1, where zero is associated with black and 1 is associated with white. As we move from the input layer to the hidden layers, these values are transformed by mathematical

functions that are used to identify specific features within an image. The number associated with each neuron dictates whether that neuron is activated or "lit up". In this case, higher numbers trigger a neuron to be activated, which implies that the algorithm detects a specific pattern. The right side of Figure 2 shows just two hidden layers for simplicity of illustration. From the input layer comprising 64 neurons of grayscale values, the first hidden layer looks for horizontal lines while the second hidden layer looks for vertical lines. These hidden layers then categorize the feature they have detected into one of the 10 numerical digits in the final output layer.

How hidden layers perform is critical to the success of the algorithm in accomplishing the vision-based task at hand. There are several variants of a neural network that can be used to make the hidden layers behave differently. One of them is a convolutional neural network (CNN), a type of deep-learning algorithm that can be applied to analyzing imagery, including satellite imagery.

Understanding Convolutional Neural Networks

In a CNN, a convolutional layer is the primary layer from which features within input images are extracted. Neural networks have a structure which connects each neuron to all neurons in the previous layer (Figure 2). Within a CNN, however, neurons in a layer are connected to only those which are spatially close, or have significant relationship with, in the previous layer. This process enables the CNN learn from very high dimensional data.

To illustrate the concept of convolution using the ongoing example, let us assume that there are four filters being used in the convolutional layer and the objective of each filter is to look for different features within the image of the handwritten "7" (Figure 3). In this case, each of the four filters is looking for a specific type of edge. The first filter is looking for top

horizontal edges as indicated by the brightest pixel, while the second filter is looking for left vertical edges. The third and fourth filters look for bottom horizontal edges and right vertical edges, respectively.

The CNN slides or "convolves" over the input image, using each of the four filters individually. During this convolution, each filter looks at every group of 9 pixels that are clustered next to each other. Visually, the output of this process might be represented by the third row of Figure 3. High values are displayed as white and low values as black, but they actually represent the spatial closeness (or relationship) between the original image and the feature being assessed. As the convolutional layers are reproduced and multiplied, the filters reach deeper into the CNN and are able to detect more sophisticated patterns.

As the number of convolutional layers increases, the number of parameters that need to be estimated also increases. However, the number of parameters can

Figure 3: Neural Network Filters to Detect Vertical and Horizontal Lines

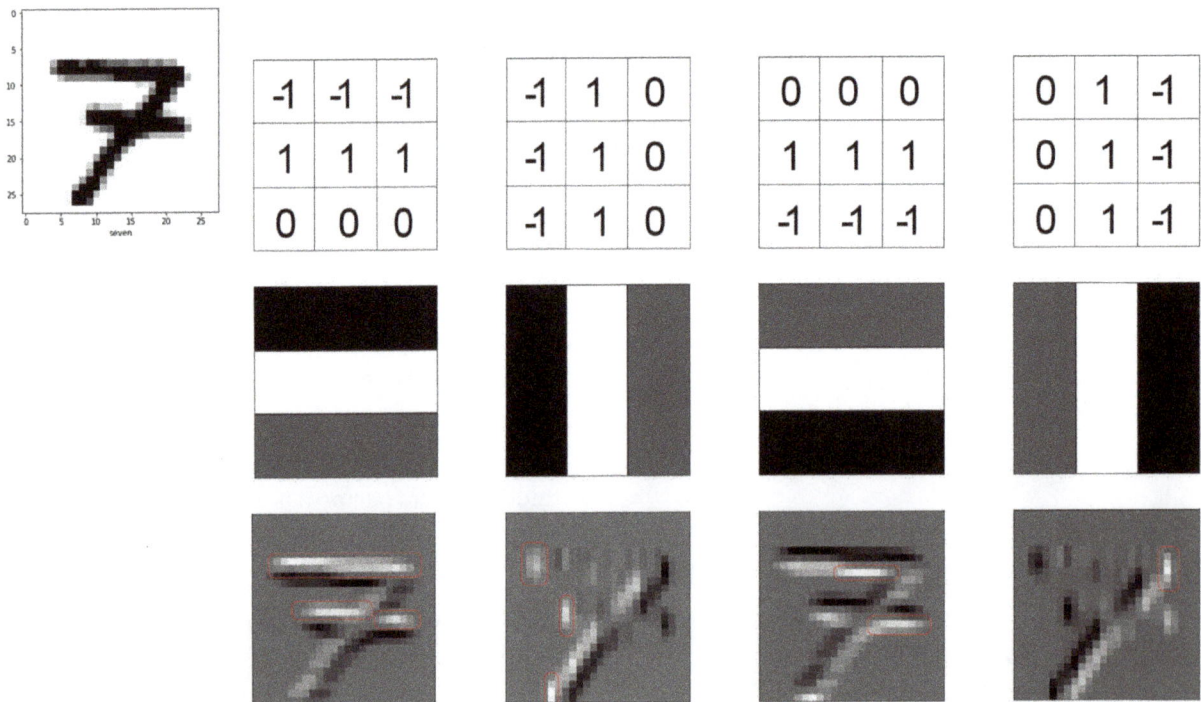

Source: Graphics generated by study team based on YouTube videos by 3blue1brown entitled "But what is a Neural Network? | Deep learning, chapter 1" and Deeplizard entitled "Convolutional Neural Networks (CNN) explained".

be reduced by removing information which are less useful. For instance, if it is useful to identify a feature at some spatial position, then it should also be useful to identify it at a different position. Thus, the position of the feature is not important in its identification. This is called parameter sharing and it reduces the computational complexity of the image analysis (Dai, et al. 2020).

The concept of pooling is another building block of a CNN. Image classification tasks are often complicated by the fact that classification is sensitive to the location of specific features within an input image. Downsampling (compressing an image's spatial information) is one approach to address this sensitivity because downsampled maps are considered more flexible to changes in the location of a specific feature within an image. Pooling layers is a way to downsample an input image. After creating a convolutional layer, it is common practice to insert pooling layers to reduce the data's spatial size, reducing the number of parameters and the computational complexity of the image analysis (Yamashita et al. 2018).

Like most variants of neural networks, a CNN is designed to cope with the large amounts of unstructured pixelized data that are contained in most digital images. One advantage of using a CNN over other types of neural networks is that it is more computationally efficient in filtering important features within an image, without any human supervision (Yamashita et al. 2018). By using special convolution, parameter sharing, and pooling operations, CNN models can be implemented on virtually any digital device, making them attractive for a wide range of data analysis purposes (Dai et al. 2020; Yamashita et al. 2018).

Outlining Data Requirements for the Feasibility Study

Figure 4 outlines a road map of the methodology used by Jean et al. (2016) to predict poverty by analyzing light data acquired from satellite imagery. By following this road map, more detailed analysis of the methodology can be applied to specific datasets from the Philippines and Thailand, which forms the basis of the feasibility study conducted for this supplement. To test the methodology in an accurate manner, three critical inputs were required: (i) daytime satellite imagery, (ii) data on night lights, and (iii) poverty statistics.

Daytime satellite imagery

Daytime satellite images are the first of three primary data requirements of the methodology used in this study. There are several possible sources of satellite imagery, with varying resolution and accessibility, whether publicly accessible or in proprietary libraries (Appendix 2).

The study of Jean et al. (2016) made use of satellite images from Google Static Maps, with 2-meter resolutions. In this study, however, publicly accessible images from Landsat 8 (30-meter resolutions reduced to 15-meter resolutions) and Sentinel 2 (10-meter resolutions) were utilized. This allowed researchers to assess whether or not using publicly accessible satellite images with lower resolutions would compromise the original approach proposed, and outcomes achieved, by Jean et al. To maximize budgetary resources, it is recommended that NSOs, when conducting similar exploratory studies, use lower resolution satellite images that are publicly accessible, instead of higher resolution proprietary images that may be expensive to procure on an ongoing basis.

Satellite images are taken every several days. One of the intermediate steps undertaken while preparing the satellite images was to collect cloud-free daytime images that covered the entirety of both the Philippines and Thailand. This process entailed running an algorithm to select the best daytime images falling within an acceptable cloudiness or cloud cover during the time period of the study. The cloudiness threshold was determined by experimenting until the algorithm produced a composite image for the whole country with the least amount of cloud cover. Although it is ideal to set a low cloudiness threshold, it is important

Figure 4: Road Map of Methodology for Predicting Poverty Using Satellite Imagery

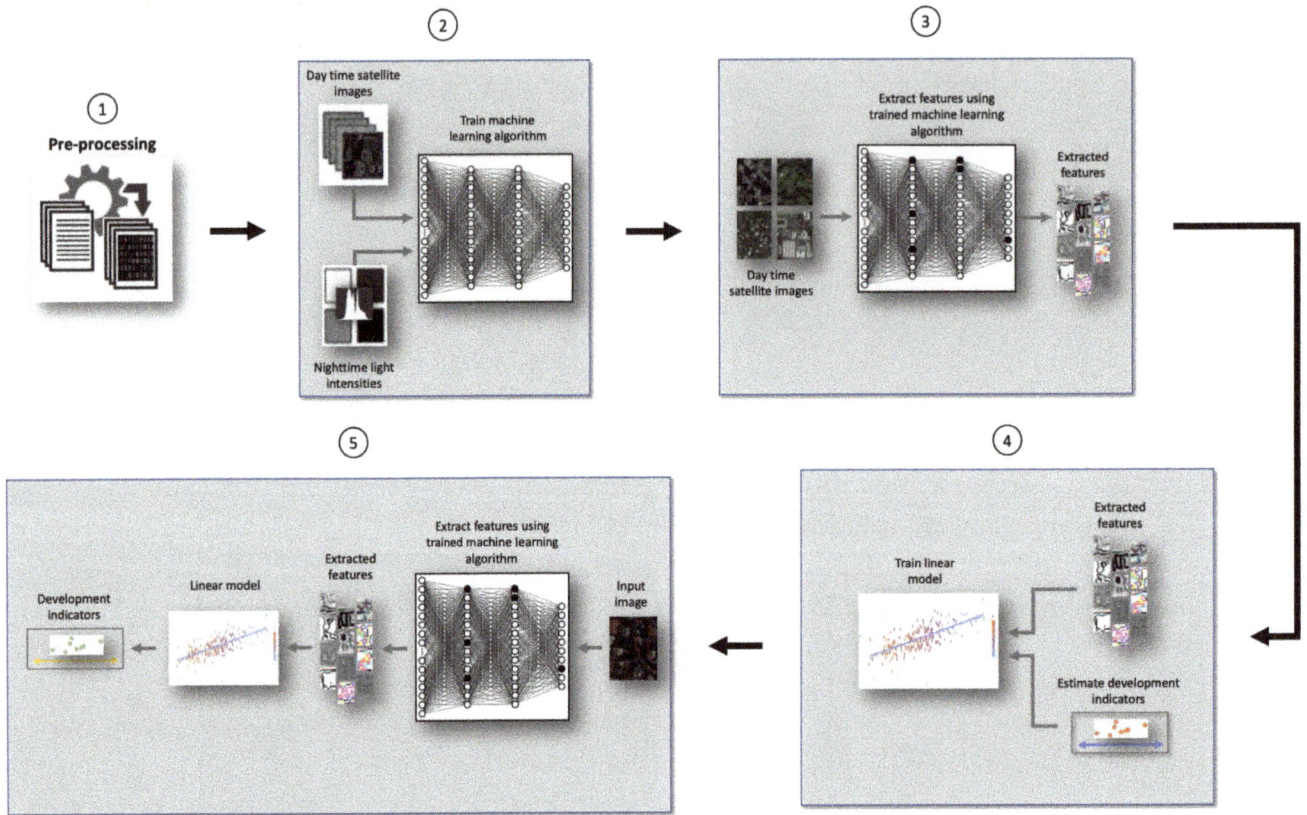

Notes: The procedure requires three types of data: geographically disaggregated poverty statistics, daytime satellite imagery, and images of earth at night. After preprocessing and cleaning these data, Step 2 trains an algorithm to classify (daytime) satellite images into different classes of night light intensity. Step 3 extracts the image features of the last layer of the trained algorithm. In Step 4, the image features are averaged so the spaces enclosed in grids correspond to the level at which poverty-labelled images are available. These are regressed using the target variable of the survey to find the relationship between features and the target variable. Step 5 summarizes the full pipeline from image to the target variable, as described in Steps 2 to 4.
Source: Graphics generated by the study team.

to note that setting a very low threshold could lead to having several areas with missing images because they are unable to meet the threshold set.

The use of "pansharpening" was another intermediate data preparation step undertaken to enhance the resolution of the Landsat 8 images. Pansharpening combines higher resolution panchromatic images (black and white but sensitive to colours) with lower resolution multispectral band images. The process, as illustrated in Figure 5, produces a single red, green, blue (RGB) color, multiband image at the higher resolution of the panchromatic image. From the original 30-meter resolutions, pansharpening was able to produce 15-meter resolutions for the Landsat images.

Most of the data preparation steps were implemented using Earth Engine, a tool developed by Google and featuring a catalogue of satellite imagery and geospatial datasets that runs into multiple petabytes (1 petabyte = 1,000 terabytes or 1,000,000 gigabytes). Earth Engine, which runs on Google's servers, has planetary-scale analysis capabilities. Geospatial Data Abstraction Library, a translator library for raster and vector geospatial data formats, was utilized for cropping images and converting them into appropriate data formats.

Figure 5: Pansharpening Images to Improve Their Resolution

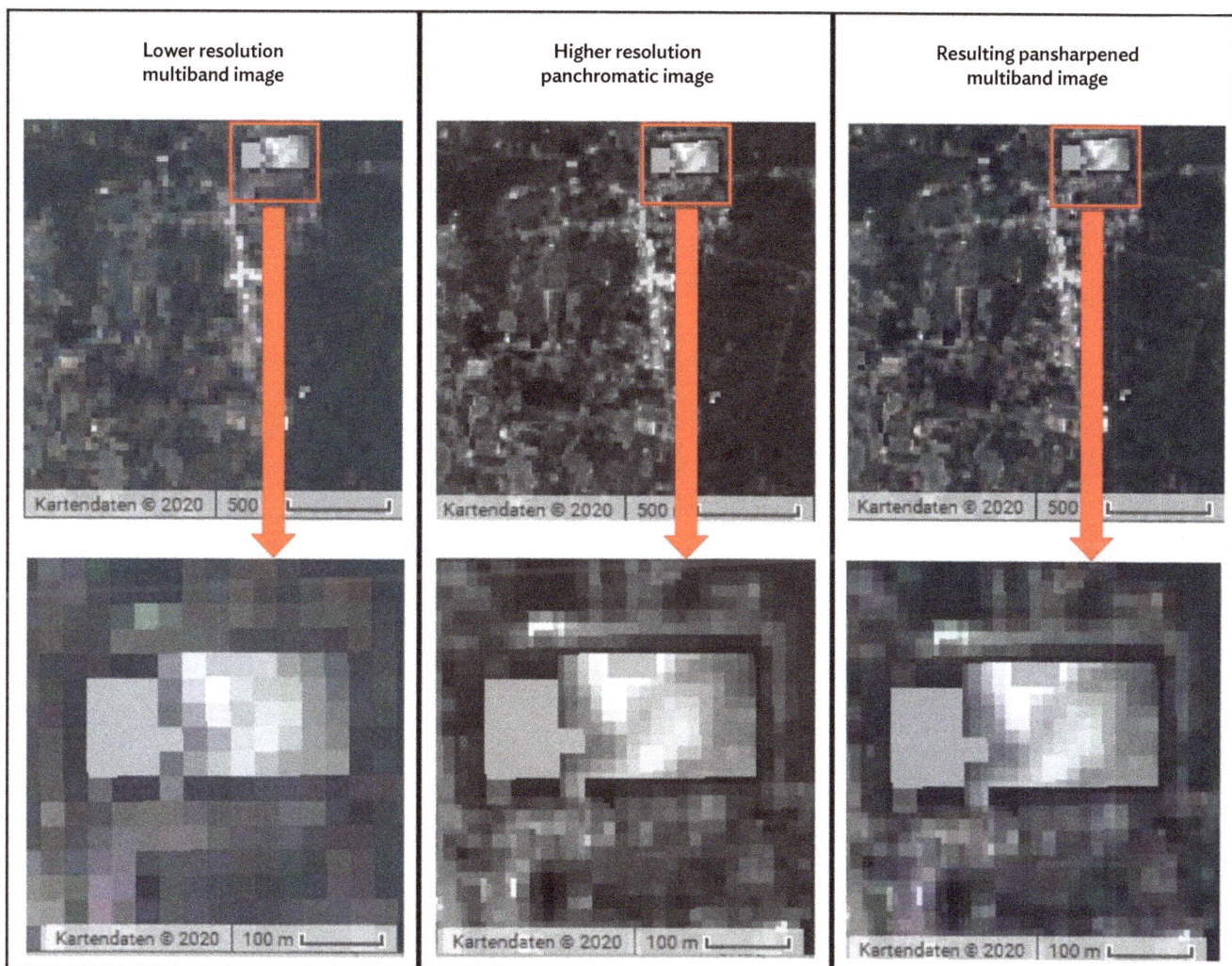

Note: These images were taken over Pueai Noi, Pueai Noi District, Thailand.
Source: Google Earth Engine.

Data on night lights

The second primary data requirement for this study is information on the intensity of night lights across the Philippines and Thailand. Data on night lights were downloaded from the Visible Infrared Imaging Radiometer Suite, which provides publicly accessible earth observation images taken at night for the entire globe. A cloud-free average radiance value was used to filter out the effects of fires and other transitory events as well as irrelevant background, while unlit areas were set to zero.

Since the Visible Infrared Imaging Radiometer Suite publishes monthly composite images (except for a few years when they also published annual composite data), custom year composites were created out of published monthly composite images (Figure 6). These custom year composites aligned with the objective of providing annual poverty statistics for specific years. The median of monthly values was calculated to minimize the effect of outliers. Additional data processing was undertaken to ensure that the resolution of night light data aligned with that of daytime satellite imagery.

Figure 6: Night Light Image Tiles for the Philippines and Thailand

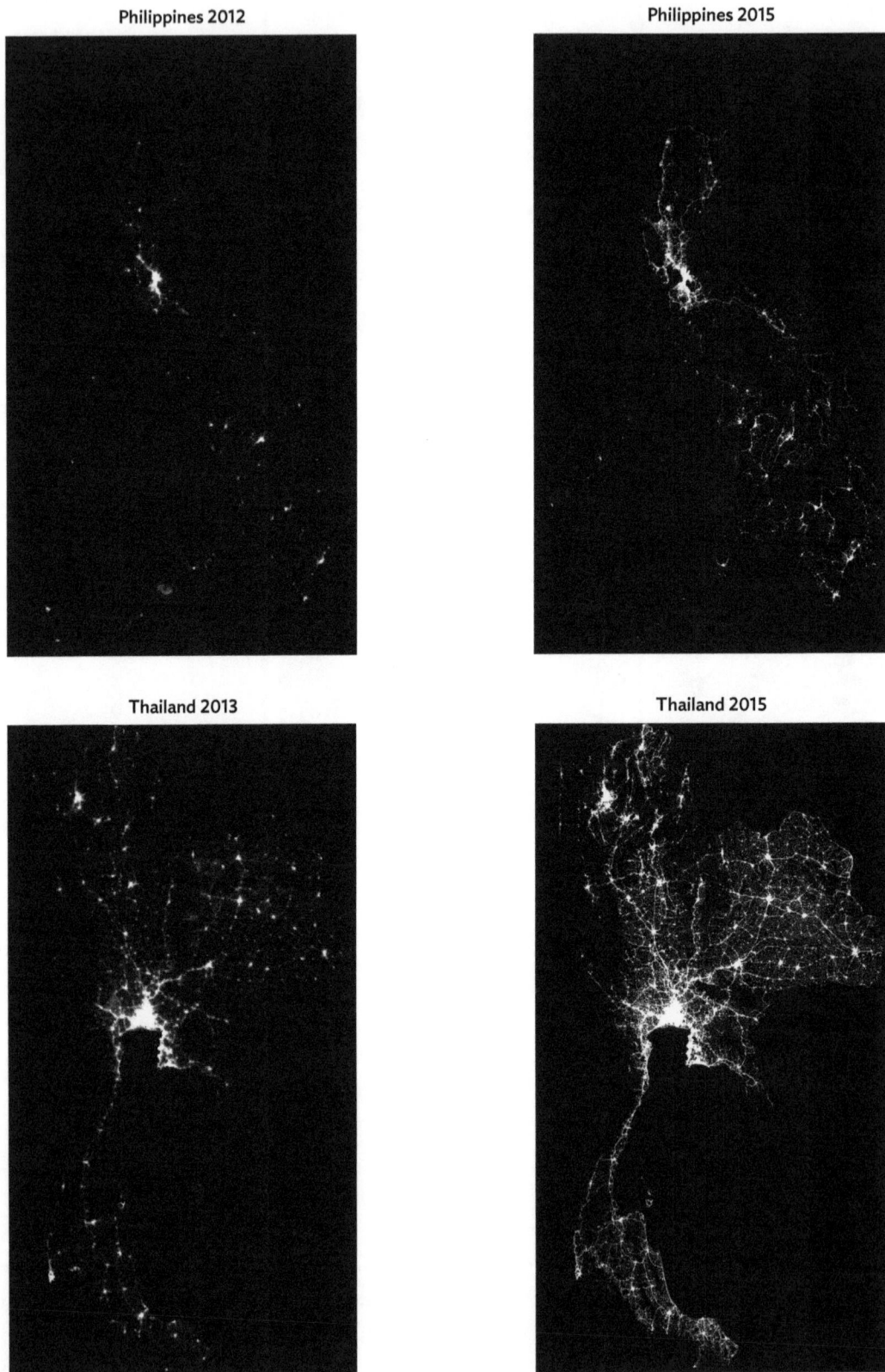

Philippines 2012

Philippines 2015

Thailand 2013

Thailand 2015

Note: These images show the annual composite distribution of night lights in the Philippines and Thailand.
Source: Visible Infrared Imaging Radiometer Suite

Actual values for the intensity of night lights were clustered into discrete groups or classes. This approach is consistent with the strategy adopted by Jean et al. (2016). Correspondingly, a Gaussian mixture model for clustering the values of night light intensity was also employed. In general, a Gaussian model assumes that the distribution of night light intensity comes from the mixture of "k" underlying normal or Gaussian distributions. The histogram of the radiance values was examined to determine the set of normal distributions that best fit the data.[5]

Poverty statistics

The third data requirement for this study is an indicator of economic well-being.[6] The Philippine Statistics Authority (PSA) and the National Statistical Office of Thailand (NSO) implemented a small area estimation (SAE) technique based on the Elbers, Lanjouw, and Lanjouw (ELL) poverty mapping method popularized by the World Bank. As discussed earlier in this supplement, the ELL method entails matching covariates that are common in both the survey and census datasets. This means that expenditure or income models are developed from the survey data and applied to the census data to generate predicted

values of expenditure or income for particular years. The predicted values are then compared with official poverty lines to calculate poverty measures at detailed geographic levels.

This study used small area poverty estimates[7] available for more than 1,600 municipalities and cities in the Philippines for the years 2012 and 2015, and for more than 7,000 tambons (townships)[8] in Thailand for the years 2013 and 2015. These available estimates were, however, not sufficiently granular to predict poverty at the most specific geographic level in each country and to enable more precise poverty-targeting measures. The lowest level of geographic unit in the Philippines is the barangay (the native Filipino term for village), while in Thailand it is the village. However, further geographic disaggregation may result in even less reliable poverty estimates than those achieved for some municipalities and tambons, which show high coefficients of variation. From this point forward in the supplement, the small area poverty estimates used will be referred to as government-published estimates.[9] Figure 7 illustrates the distribution of poverty data used in this study.

[5] The Gaussian mixture model does not always guarantee accurate results. Sometimes, the approach is unable to create optimal clusters. In such cases, the optimal cluster must be determined through intuitive approaches or experimentation. In doing so, it is important to create appropriate clusters such that the smallest cluster has at least a few hundred values to meet machine learning requirements. In this study, three clusters were formed for both countries.

[6] In the study by Jean et al. (2016), which used data from African countries, village-level data were consumption expenditure derived from the Living Standards Measurement Survey and household assets scores derived from the Demographic and Health Survey. However, most household surveys conducted in Asia and the Pacific do not provide reliable estimates at the village level.

[7] In the case of the Philippines, per capita household income, which is the variable of interest, is available from the Family Income and Expenditure Survey. Auxiliary variables from the Family Income and Expenditure Survey, Labor Force Survey, and Census of Population and Housing are combined to build a per capita income model in log terms. The survey-obtainable explanatory variables pertain to household or individual variables such as educational attainment of the household head, while census-derivable explanatory variables refer to municipal or barangay level variables such as the average family size in a barangay. The covariates in the regression model are strategically chosen such that they have comparable definitions, consistent summary statistics such as mean values, and are available in both the survey and the census. The predicted household per capita incomes are then compared with official provincial poverty lines to compute the small area poverty estimates (PSA 2005; PSA 2016). For the 2015 small area poverty estimates in the Philippines, the poverty rates range from 0.7% to 78.5%, while the coefficients of variation of resulting poverty estimates range from 2.9% to 55.5%. Thailand follows the same SAE methodology as the Philippines, but uses per capita household expenditure, which is derived from the Household Socio-Economic Survey, as the variable of interest. Auxiliary information from the Household Socio-Economic Survey and the Census of Population and Housing are combined to build a per capita household expenditure model. The model includes household assets as well as demographic, education, occupational, and other variables that are potentially correlated with expenditure. The predicted household per capita expenditures are then compared with official poverty lines to calculate the small area poverty estimates. For this study, the 2013 and 2015 small area poverty estimates for more than 7,000 tambons in Thailand were used. For the 2015 small area poverty estimates in Thailand, the poverty rates range from 0% to 99.7%

[8] The area of municipalities or cities in the Philippines ranges from 3.0 million square meters (m2) to 2.1 billion m2, with a median size of 112.1 million m2. Meanwhile, the area of tambons ranges from 616 m2 to 2.1 billion m2, with a median size of 40.8 million m2.

[9] In general, official statistics on poverty are not based on small area estimates and are instead directly estimated from surveys conducted by NSOs. In such cases, official statistics are published at higher aggregation levels.

Figure 7: Distribution of Poverty Rates in the Philippines and Thailand

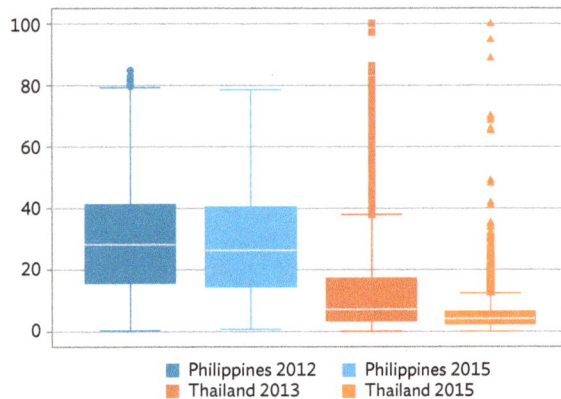

- Philippines 2012
- Philippines 2015
- Thailand 2013
- Thailand 2015

Source: Calculations and graphics generated by the study team.

The objective of this study is to provide poverty estimates that are more granular than the currently available government-published estimates. From a policy perspective, having more granular information could facilitate more specific and efficient poverty reduction strategies and resource allocation. Such granularity may be achieved by developing an algorithm that can predict poverty by analysing satellite images

to detect features associated with particular aspects of economic development.

Applying a Convolutional Neural Network to Poverty Prediction

The methodological principles of a CNN can be extended to predict poverty. The main objective is to use a transfer learning technique, whereby a CNN is first taught to predict the intensity of night lights based on features in daytime satellite images, then to use those features for predicting poverty.[10]

The input data for this study were obtained using georeferenced and tagged image files sourced from Landsat 8 and Sentinel 2. These image files are stored as three-dimensional arrays, with each pixel represented in red, green, and blue color bands (Figure 8).[11]

Instead of developing a CNN algorithm from scratch, the study employed an off-the-shelf CNN called

Figure 8: Image Color Bands within a Georeferenced Image File

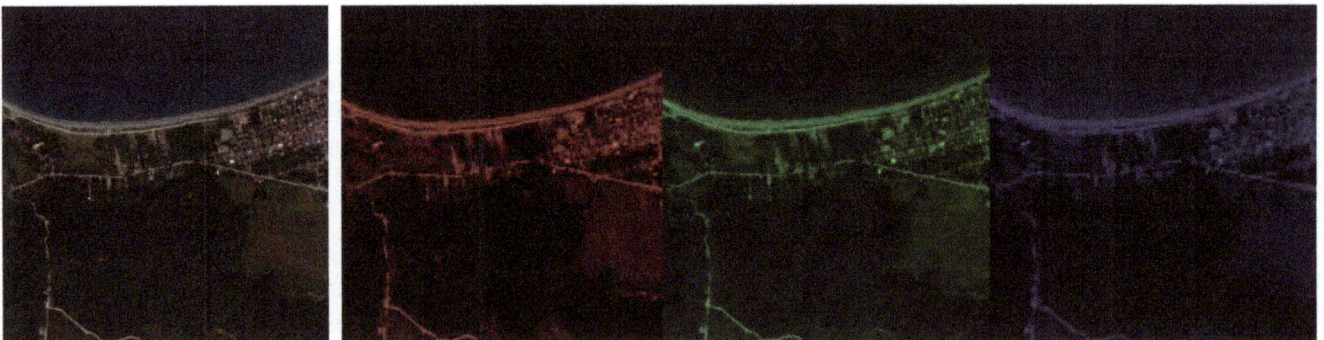

Note: These images were taken over the Philippines (Claveria, Cagayan).
Source: Sentinel 2 satellite

---

[10] The available literature covers various transfer learning methods (Pan and Yang 2018). Technically speaking, two instances of transfer learning are employed. The first instance is the use of a pretrained image classifier, rather than starting out with random parameters in a CNN. The pretrained model has been trained on a large image database. The basic features of the early layers such as edges, corners, and other geometric patterns are generally helpful for any kind of image classification. Therefore, by using a CNN that already knows how to detect such features, we can greatly reduce the computation time.

[11] In principle, satellites have multiple bands, including infrared. The authors of this feasibility study focussed on RGB color bands only because the CNN had been pretrained on regular RGB images (through ImageNet).

ResNet34. This algorithm has been pretrained using the ImageNet database[12] to ensure that it is capable of identifying simple features. Steps were then taken to train deeper layers of the CNN to recognize more complex features of the daytime satellite imagery, predict the intensity of night lights, and, eventually, estimate poverty levels.

During the training process, different CNN specifications were applied to find an optimal network structure. Throughout the training process, several validation checks were conducted. The images were regularly examined and those that yielded the highest number of prediction errors as determined by a chosen loss function during the training were checked. Images with low quality i.e., too much clouds or no land or urban areas recognizable, were isolated because they can contaminate the input dataset. High levels of loss being observed in these 'low quality' images signalled that the training process was working well in terms of accurately identifying valid features within the satellite images. Figure 9 shows three examples of images that were isolated during validation. As these images were visually clouded and no land or urban areas were recognizable, the CNN could not correctly predict the class of night lights and therefore trained on incorrect features. Most likely, the poor image quality was caused by weather disturbances or camera issues. However, regardless of the reason, such images were removed from further training to avoid contaminating the input data set.

Another way to fine-tune the training process is to monitor the confusion matrix, which shows the number of accurate and inaccurate predictions, then to use an appropriate loss function to mitigate imbalanced prediction classes. The feasibility study team also used a weighted cross entropy loss function—a concept explained further in Appendix 1—because it penalizes the model more for wrong predictions of low frequency (high night light images) based on weights.[13] This approach prevents the CNN from always predicting low night light classes because they have the most samples.

Figure 9: Low-Quality Satellite Images Isolated from Training

Note: These images were taken over the Laguna Lake Philippines.
Source: Landsat 8 satellite.

---

[12] In this context, pre-training refers to using an algorithm that can already detect image features, such as lines, edges, etc., instead of developing an algorithm from scratch. The algorithm is trained on a wide range of images. Many features relevant for general image classification tasks overlap, regardless of the source of the image. The database used for pre-training in this study, ImageNet, is regarded as a solid benchmark performer in computer vision predictions.

[13] A loss function is used to evaluate how well an algorithm performs a target task. A cross entropy function is commonly used in an image classification task.

In the images analyzed for this study, more than 500 features were extracted from the last layer of the CNN.[14] A sample of these features, and how they were correlated with intensity of night lights, is presented in Figure 10.

Extracting Features from the Convolutional Neural Network

After implementing the CNN, the next step in the study was to extract the features within the satellite images that were used in predicting the night light intensity. This was a fairly straightforward process as these features were viewed numerically by the CNN as complex mathematical functions. To simplify the illustration of the process, Figure 11 demonstrates a hypothetical case where each geographical area has two input images.

From each image, the CNN's final layer produces *"k"* feature values. With two input images for each area, we can represent the values of the CNN's final layer as *"θ_{i1}"* for the first input image and *"θ_{i2}"* for the second input image. To derive the aggregated feature average, we simply take the mean of θ_{i1} and θ_{i2}.

Since the primary objective of the study was to predict poverty, the average of the mathematical functions was taken, then aggregated to the same geographical level for which the government-published poverty estimates were compiled. For Thailand, data were aggregated at the tambon level for 2013 and 2015, while for the Philippines data were aggregated to the municipality or city level for 2012 and 2015.

Figure 10: Examples of Features Extracted from the Convolutional Neural Network

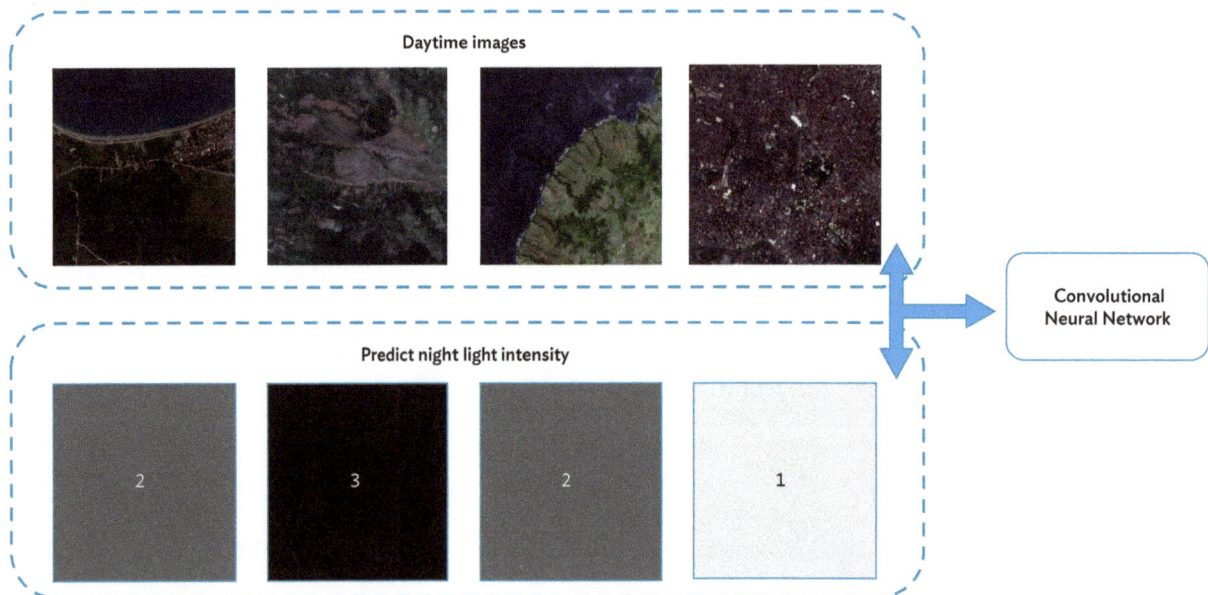

Note: These images were taken over the Philippines; from left to right: (Claveria, Cagayan), (Bagac, Bataan), (Itbayat, Batanes) and (Sta Cruz, Manila).
Source: Sentinel 2 satellite.

---

[14] To implement the CNN, the study's authors used specialist libraries that can be built upon to execute tasks that require the application of deep-learning methods (Appendix 1). In this case, Fastai, which is built on PyTorch, was used. One of the advantages of using PyTorch is that it is a free and open-source software, developed by Facebook's artificial intelligence research lab.

Figure 11: Extracting a Convolutional Neural Network's Output Layer

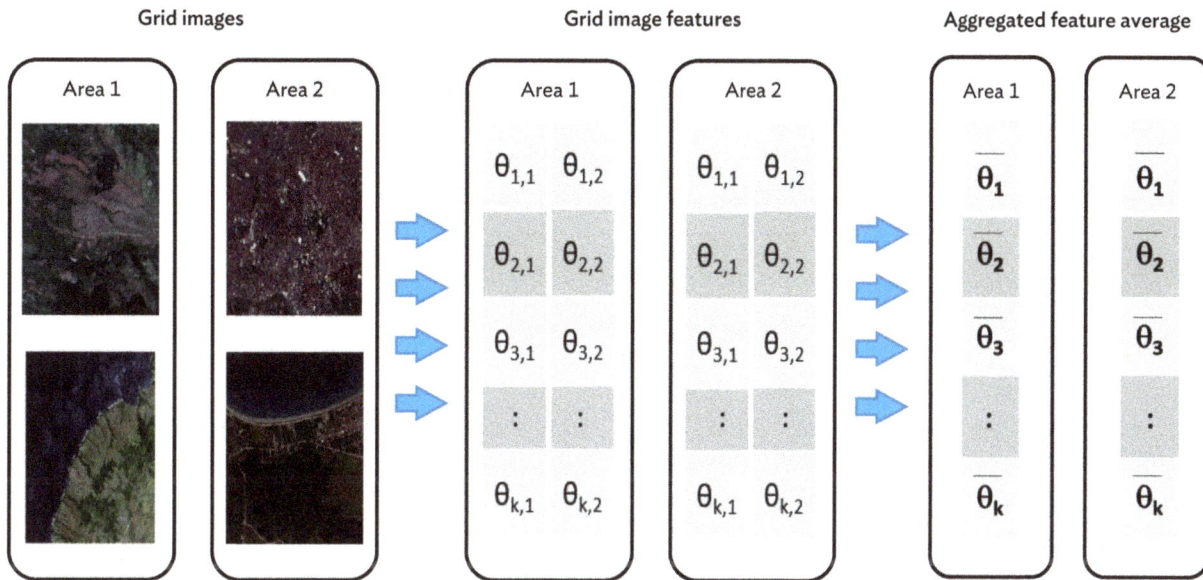

Note: These images were taken over the Philippines; from upper left to bottom right: (Bagac, Bataan), (Sta Cruz, Manila) (Itbayat, Batanes) and (Claveria, Cagayan).
Source: Sentinel 2 satellite.

Predicting Poverty from Features Using Ridge Regression Models

The researchers next set out to regress the poverty rates on the aggregated data for Thailand and the Philippines.

In choosing a regression technique, the authors of the study examined the feasibility of using alternative estimation techniques such as the ordinary least squares (OLS) method, which tends to find the best linear unbiased estimator. In general, OLS finds coefficients that best fit a given estimation sample. It uses every covariate in a linear specification. However, when the number of covariates is large, there could

be overfitting because OLS will find coefficients that fit the training data almost perfectly, but often fail to fit or predict additional data. A ridge regression is a good alternative to OLS as it addresses the issues of OLS by penalizing large coefficients to shrink unimportant ones toward zero. For this reason, the researchers decided to use ridge regression.[15] The resulting coefficients of the ridge regression model are then applied to satellite image tiles with a 4-kilometer by 4-kilometer resolution to provide more granular poverty estimates.[16]

It is important to note that for each combination of country and year, the researchers set aside 10% of the areas for which government-published estimates of poverty were available.[17] These areas make up the validation set. Both the CNN and the ridge regression

---

[15] Alternative modeling strategies—such as random forest estimation, support vector regression, and others—can also be considered (Puttanapong et al. 2020).

[16] The extent of granularity depends on the resolution of images used and the level of disaggregation of poverty data that served as inputs. Details are provided in Hofer et al. Forthcoming.

[17] In the existing literature, there is hardly an agreement on what is the optimal allocation of splitting data between training and validation (Xu and Goodacre 2018). If an input data set has few data points, increasing the allocation for validation will significantly reduce the amount of data that can be used for training and therefore, may yield unreliable results.

training models used additional training and test splits, independent of each other. In particular, 10 fold cross validation was used to tune hyperparameters. These training sets were taken after setting aside the 10% validation set.

Outlining the Key Findings of the Feasibility Study[18]

As discussed, the first step of this study's poverty prediction methodology was to train a CNN to predict the intensity of lights at night using daytime imagery. Tables 2 and 3 present the confusion matrixes calculated from the predictions of the CNN's final layer. The y-axis shows the actual group based on intensity of night lights, while the x-axis shows the predicted group based on the CNN. The number inside each cell corresponds to the number of satellite images from the validation set.

Table 2: Summary of Poverty Prediction Results using Confusion Matrixes, Thailand

		Predicted (2013)				Predicted (2015)		
		1	2	3		1	2	3
Actual	1	2,561	181	0	Actual	2,531	146	8
	2	224	437	37		224	250	26
	3	1	71	104		14	47	80

Overall accuracies: THA 2013 = 0.85785, THA 2015 = 0.85219.

THA = Thailand.
Source: Calculations generated by the study team.

Table 3: Summary of Poverty Prediction Results using Confusion Matrixes, Philippines

		Predicted (2012)				Predicted (2015)		
		1	2	3		1	2	3
Actual	1	1,299	24	2	Actual	1,170	18	0
	2	36	32	6		50	38	2
	3	4	12	21		3	13	29

Overall accuracies: PHI 2012 = 0.9415, PHI 2015 = 0.935.

PHI = Philippines
Source: Calculations generated by the study team.

Comparing the overall prediction accuracy—calculated as the number of images correctly predicted divided by the total number of images across rows—the results suggest that the CNN performed well in correctly predicting lower levels of night light intensity in both the Philippines and Thailand for the specific years considered in this study. A possible explanation for this is that the features associated with low levels of night light intensity are more homogenous, making it easier for the algorithm to make accurate predictions.

Furthermore, prediction accuracy is better in the Philippines than in Thailand. This may be explained by the difference in the distribution of night-light values in the two countries. As the Philippines has lower and sparser night-light values, it is easier for the model to correctly predict low night-light classes whereby no, or only a few, man-made structures are visible, leading to higher prediction accuracy.

Prediction of night light intensity is only an intermediate step to extract the features of satellite images that are needed to estimate a ridge regression model designed for poverty prediction. Several validation tasks were performed to numerically assess the predictive performance of the adopted method.

The first validation metric was based on the root mean square error (RMSE), calculated at the city or municipal level for the Philippines, and at the tambon level for Thailand. Since the original poverty predictions produced by the CNN are expressed at the grid level, the weighted averages of grid-level poverty rates (weighted by population estimates of the grids) were derived to express all estimates at the city, municipality, or tambon level (Box 4).

---

[18] Discussion of other technical findings of this study can be found in Hofer et al. Forthcoming.

Box 4: Compiling Grid-Level Estimates of Poverty Head Count

Apart from predicting poverty rates at the grid level, the study's authors also estimated the number of poor individuals or the "poverty head count" in areas of the Philippines and Thailand. The first step entailed estimating grid-level population size, then multiplying those estimates with the poverty rates derived from the ridge regression of the convolutional neural network, to yield grid-level estimates of the poverty head count.

To estimate grid-level population size, country-specific census data were used and these were matched to administrative boundaries (derived from geographic information systems) for the tambons of Thailand as well as cities and/or municipalities in the Philippines. These administrative levels of data provided the finest level administrative unit available at the time of analysis.

The "random forest" model was used with log population density from the census as the response variable, while the covariates were derived from geospatial data. Compiling potential covariates was guided by relevant literature. Since several studies showed that population distribution was usually highly correlated with land cover types, land cover data in the compiled list of potential covariates were included in the model. The figure below illustrates the relationship between population distribution and a specific land cover class corresponding to artificial surfaces and associated areas. The land cover class is shown in the left panel. On the right of the figure is a map that contains estimates of population density on the grid level in Bangkok, Thailand. The yellow portions of the map indicate a relatively high population density, while the purple portions indicate a relatively low population density.

Land Cover Class showing Artificial Surfaces and Associated Areas versus Population Density in Bangkok, 2015

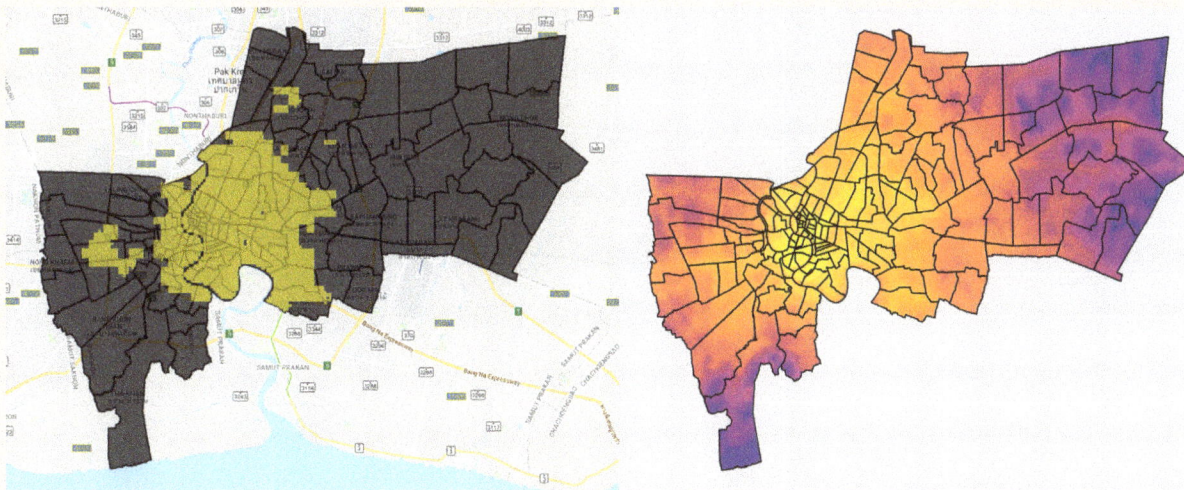

Source: Calculations and graphics generated by the study team.

GlobCover, a European Space Agency initiative aimed at developing a service capable of delivering global composites and land cover maps, served as the source of information on land cover classes. This service provides high-quality and publicly available data with good coverage for both the Philippines and Thailand. The same data source has been used in similar studies that estimated grid-level population counts (Stevens et al. 2015). The land cover data were complemented by digital elevation data, and the derived slope estimate was based on HydroSHEDS data, net primary production data derived from the Moderate Resolution Imaging Spectroradiometer, weather data from World Climate, data on intensity of night lights from the Visible Infrared Imaging Radiometer Suite, and other map features from OpenStreetMap.

(continued on next page)

Box 4: Compiling Grid-Level Estimates of Poverty Head Count *(continued)*

The random forest model was chosen as the modeling framework because of the various advantages it offers. First, this model can deal with large sets of explanatory data. Second, it can handle both collinearity and nonlinearity, which allows it to deal with correlations between independent variables in the input data as well as nonlinear relations between the dependent variable and its covariates. Moreover, random forest estimations offer a good balance between bias and variance. In statistics and machine learning, there is usually a trade-off between a model's bias and its variance, where neither of the two issues should become too dominant. The random forest model manages to control both bias and variance in a reasonable way. Another upside of the modelling framework is that it is resistant to overfitting. Even with a very large set of training data, the model will not only reflect the dynamics of the training information, but will be able to make accurate predictions with new input data. Furthermore, the random forest model can automatically produce measures of variable importance, indicating which covariates are most vital to obtaining accurate results. Finally, with large sets of training data, the modelling framework can produce very precise predictions.

To illustrate, the figure below shows the estimated population densities for the specific years of the study, outlining grids of 100 meters by 100 meters in Bangkok, Thailand and Manila, Philippines. To estimate population counts, the estimated population density was simply multiplied with its corresponding land area.

Random Forest Prediction of Population Density in Bangkok, 2013 and 2015
Population Density in the city of Bangkok

m = meter
Source: Calculations and graphics generated by the study team.

(continued on next page)

Table 4 suggests lower average prediction errors in Thailand. However, having lower RMSE scores in Thailand may be expected, since many tambons have similarly low poverty rates. On the other hand, in years when Landsat images were used, generally higher error bands were observed, especially in Thailand. This may be attributed to the fact that Sentinel images have slightly better resolution than Landsat images.

Table 4: Root Mean Square Error by Country and Year		
Country/Year	Validation Set	All
PHI, 2012	17%	17%
PHI, 2015	17%	15%
THA, 2013	12%	11%
THA, 2015	4%	5%

PHI = Philippines, THA = Thailand
Source: Calculations generated by the study team.

Box 4: Compiling Grid-Level Estimates of Poverty Head Count   *(continued)*

Random Forest Prediction of Population Density in Manila, 2012 and 2015

Population Density in the city of Manila

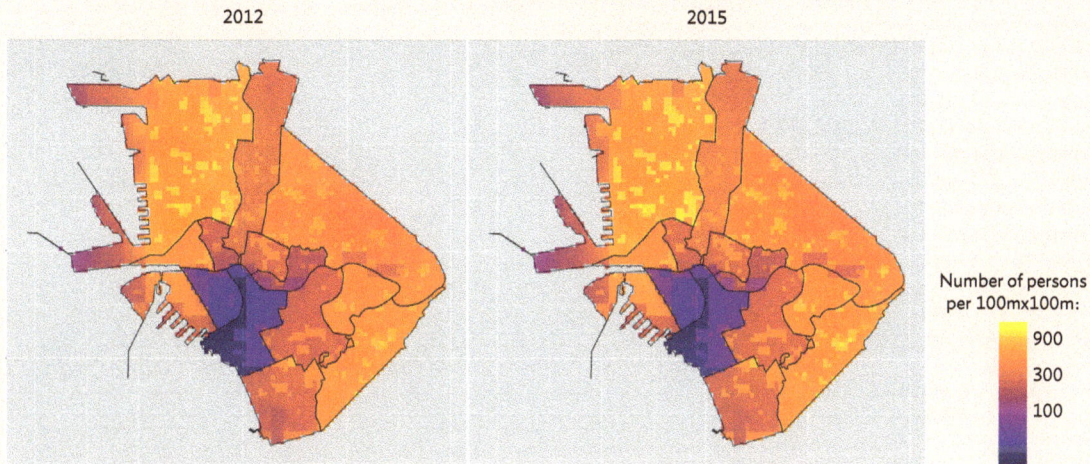

m = meter

Source: Calculations and graphics generated by the study team.

As mentioned, once the grid-level estimates of population counts were prepared, estimations of the poverty head count were generated by multiplying the grid-level population counts with the grid-level poverty rates derived earlier. However, since the size of the grid for estimates of poverty rates is larger than the size of the grid for population counts, a uniform poverty rate within each 4-kilometer by 4-kiolometer grid was assumed.

Reference

F. Stevens, et al. 2015. Disaggregating Census Data for Population Mapping Using Random Forests with Remotely-Sensed and Ancillary Data. PLoS One 10, e0107042

Scatter plots may be used as an alternative validation tool. In the scatter plot shown in Figure 12, each dot represents one city, municipality, or tambon. The x–axis contains the government-published poverty estimates for the years examined under this study, while the y–axis shows the predictions based on the machine-learning model for those same years. The blue dots represent the training set, while the red dots denote the validation set. The closer a point is to the dashed 45° line, the better the prediction. In this context, a scatter plot is an informative visual as it shows overall fit and dispersion clusters among other patterns.

Despite Thailand having lower RMSE values, Figure 12 illustrates that the machine-learning model does not perform well in predicting higher levels of poverty in Thailand. One possible reason for this is there were significantly more tambons with low poverty rates than tambons with poverty rates exceeding 20%, as shown in Figure 7. The lack of variability in the available poverty data may have contributed to the algorithm's underestimation of poverty distribution in Thailand.[19]

---

[19] Different modeling strategies were considered but the data fit did not improve significantly. As Box 5 reveals, the fit improved when the study team considered alternative dependent variables that have much larger variability than income poverty rates.

Figure 12: Scatter Plot of Published and Predicted Poverty Rates

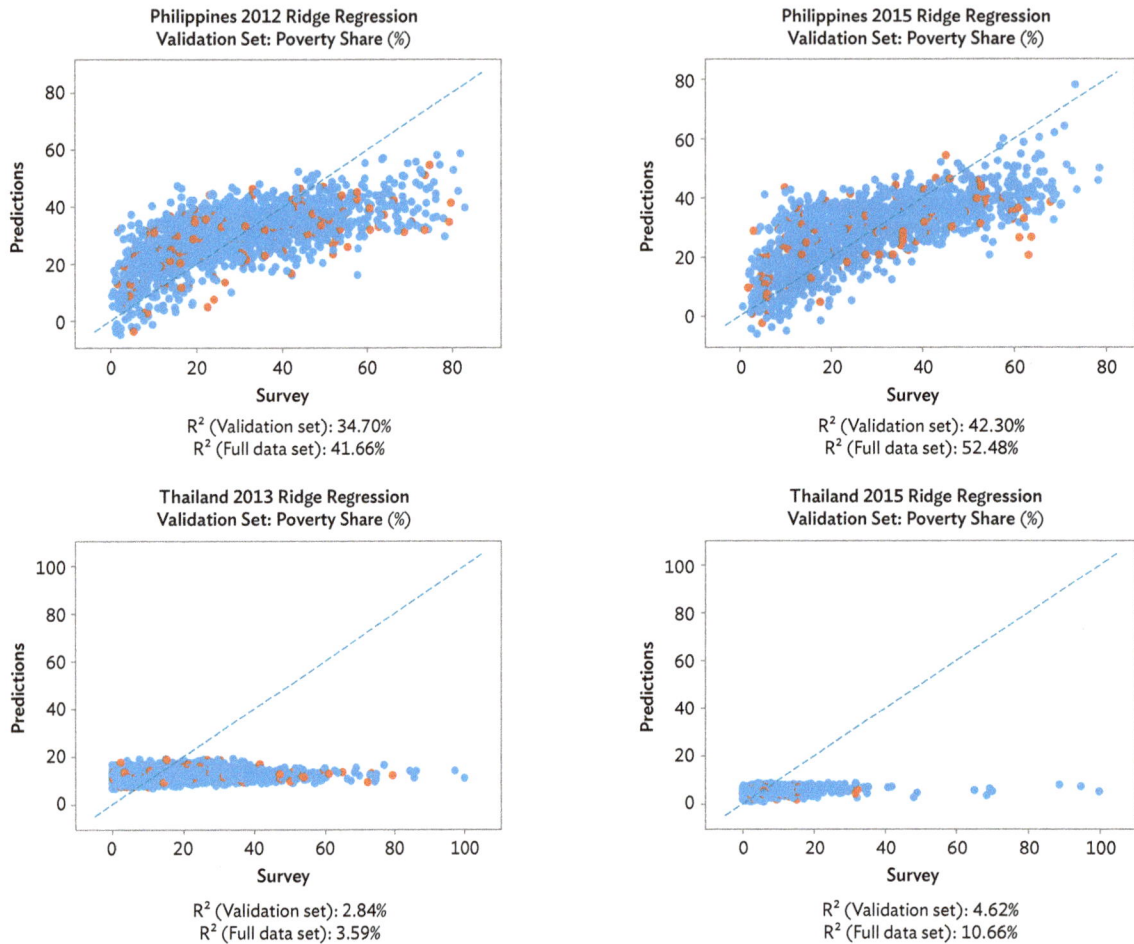

Notes: The x-axis contains the government-published poverty estimates for each year specified, while the y-axis shows the predictions based on the machine-learning model for those same years. The blue dots represent the training set, while the red dots denote the validation set.

Source: Calculations and graphics generated by the study team.

To confirm whether the distribution of the indicator of interest affects the prediction accuracy of the algorithm, other nonmonetary indicators of poverty, such as ownership of assets and a multidimensional poverty index in Thailand, were considered (Box 5). The results seem to confirm the initial hypothesis that the distribution of the indicator does affect the algorithm's prediction accuracy. In particular, it was found that the distribution of predicted values derived from the algorithm was more aligned with the distribution of the target indicator when the latter's data have a reasonable amount of variability.

Instead of estimating a ridge regression model for income poverty rates, the data was regressed on the variables described above. The predictive performance of the model is summarized in the scatter plots below. The results suggest that predictive performance is better when dealing with a variable that has a reasonable amount of variation.

Up to this point, the study has assessed the performance of the algorithm based on how far each individual poverty prediction is from its corresponding government-published poverty estimate. Nevertheless,

Box 5: Does the Algorithm's Prediction Accuracy Improve when the Indicator has more Variability?

To test the hypothesis of whether a lack of dispersion or variability in the distribution of government-published poverty estimates had an effect on the prediction accuracy of the algorithm in Thailand, the study's authors explored other metrics related to income poverty rates.

In particular, two types of alternative indicators were explored: a multidimensional poverty index (MPI) and the proportion of households owning different types of assets and durable goods. Tambon-level data on the MPI were compiled by the National Economic and Social Development Council of Thailand, following a similar methodology developed by the Oxford Poverty and Human Development Initiative (Alkire et al. 2019). At the same time, the study's authors compiled provincial-level estimates of asset and durable goods ownership, using results from the Socioeconomic Survey conducted in 2015 by the National Statistical Office of Thailand. As the figure below shows, relative to the distribution of income poverty rates in Thailand, the variability in the distribution of the MPI estimates is comparable with that of income poverty. However, the individual distributions measuring the ownership of assets and durable goods—such as house and lot, house made of light materials, big-screen televisions, washing machines, cars, cell phones, and refrigerators—have larger variability.

Plots of Multidimensional Poverty Index and Asset Ownership

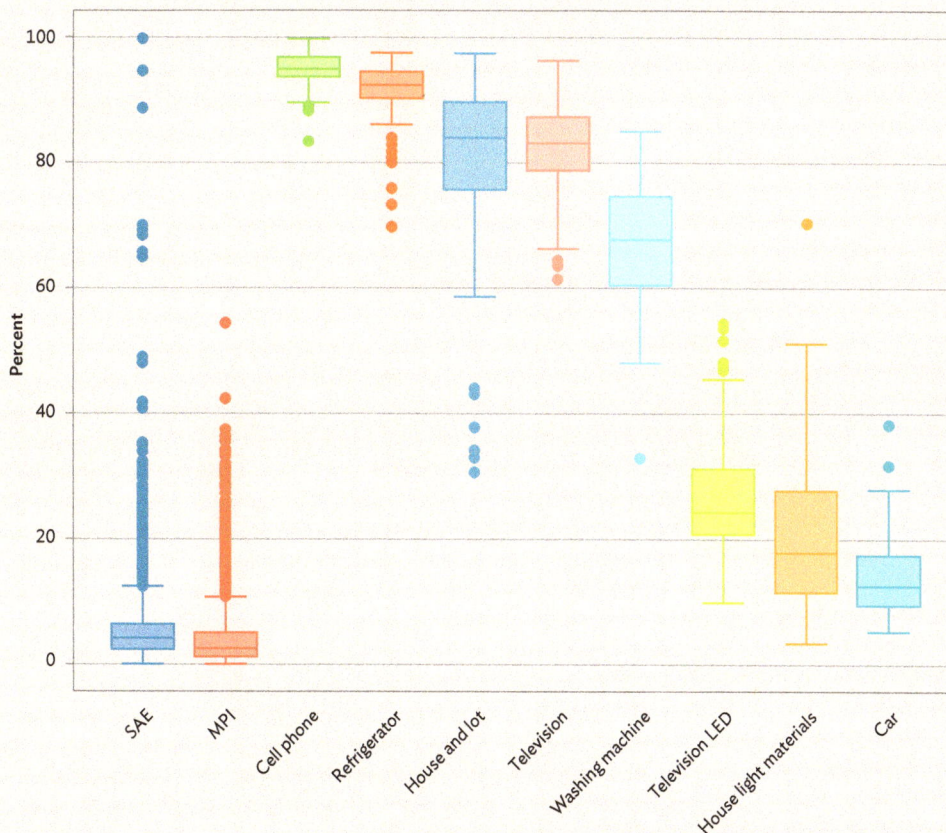

LED = light-emitting diode, MPI = multidimensional poverty index, SAE= small area estimates of poverty.
Source: Calculations and graphics generated by the study team.

(continued on next page)

Box 5: Does the Algorithm's Prediction Accuracy Improve when the Indicator has more Variability? *(continued)*

Instead of estimating a ridge regression model for income poverty rates, the data was regressed on the variables described above. The predictive performance of the model is summarized in the scatter plots below. The results suggest that predictive performance is better when dealing with a variable that has a reasonable amount of variation.

Scatter Plot of Published and Predicted Values of Alternative Variables

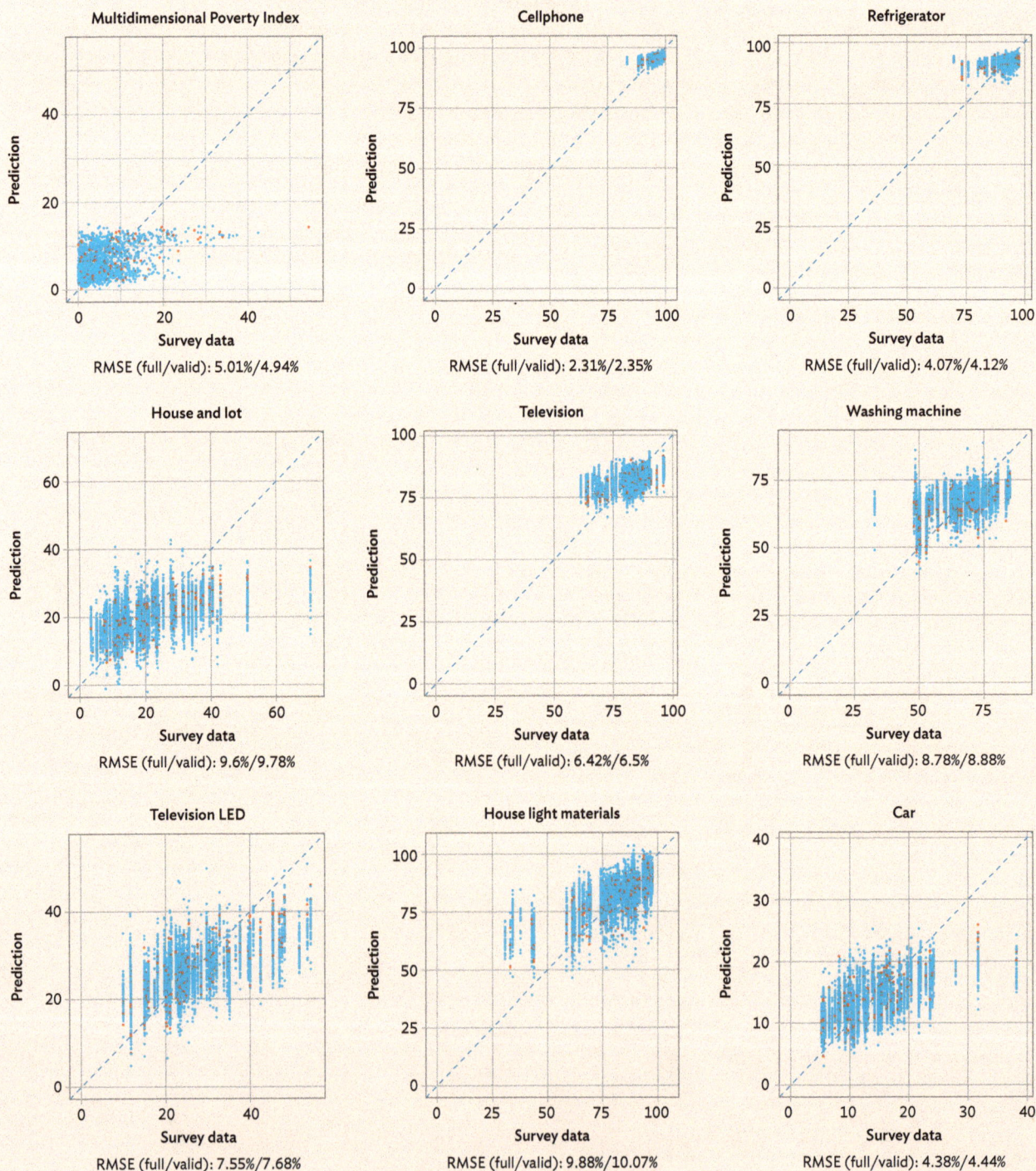

Multidimensional Poverty Index
RMSE (full/valid): 5.01%/4.94%

Cellphone
RMSE (full/valid): 2.31%/2.35%

Refrigerator
RMSE (full/valid): 4.07%/4.12%

House and lot
RMSE (full/valid): 9.6%/9.78%

Television
RMSE (full/valid): 6.42%/6.5%

Washing machine
RMSE (full/valid): 8.78%/8.88%

Television LED
RMSE (full/valid): 7.55%/7.68%

House light materials
RMSE (full/valid): 9.88%/10.07%

Car
RMSE (full/valid): 4.38%/4.44%

full = full data set; valid = validation set.
Source: Calculations and graphics generated by the study team.

it is also important to examine the spatial distribution of the poverty predictions. The poverty maps in Figure 13 indicate that the machine-learning predictions, presented at the 4-kilometer by 4-kilometer grid level, mimicked the spatial distribution of the government-published poverty estimates. In other words, in areas where government-published poverty estimates were lower or higher relative to other areas, the machine-learning predictions showed the same pattern.

However, areas with very high levels of poverty based on government-published estimates tended to be underestimated by the machine-learning model. For instance, in the northern and southern parts of the Philippines, where government-published estimates showed several areas with poverty rates exceeding 60%, the corresponding machine-learning predictions were much lower. This point echoes the findings based on the scatter plot for Thailand in Figure 13, where it was surmised that the algorithm seemed to slightly underestimate poverty in the poorest areas.

To address the issue of underestimation in the poorest areas, calibration methods can be employed. If it is assumed that government-published estimates provide an accurate picture of poverty at the level for which statistics are published (i.e., municipal or city level in the Philippines and tambon level in Thailand), machine-learning predictions can be rescaled or calibrated such that, when the grid-level predictions are aggregated at the appropriate levels, they align more closely with the government-published numbers. The calibration should preserve the distributional structure of the grid-level poverty predictions, but still pay heed to the estimates published by the government at more aggregated levels. In practice, adopting this type of

calibration may be appealing as it avoids confusion for users who traditionally rely on government estimates published by national statistics offices and other relevant government agencies, but who must also examine alternative data sources. Figure 14 shows the distribution of grid-level poverty predictions that have been calibrated for the Philippines and Thailand.

If, on the other hand, there are concerns about the reliability of the government-published estimates at the aggregate level, the uncalibrated machine-learning predictions may be used as a point of validation.[20] In particular, if the differences between the uncalibrated predictions and the government-published estimates are minimal, there may be cause to have increased confidence in the reliability of the government's poverty estimates. However, where there are more significant differences between the predictions and the estimates, further investigation may be merited.

Preparing National Statistics Offices for the Use of Big Data[21]

The objective of this study was to examine the feasibility of enhancing the compilation of poverty statistics by complementing conventional data sources with nontraditional types of data. In particular, the study looked at enhancing household survey and census data by using deep-learning methods that could analyze satellite imagery to predict poverty at granular geographic levels.[22] The results of the study are generally encouraging, but the challenge lies in scaling up this type of initiative in the future.

---

20 In general, there are several reasons why there could be concerns about the reliability of an official statistic. In the case of poverty estimation, if the statistics are directly estimated from household surveys, there is a chance that the homeless or those who do not have permanent dwellings are not captured in such surveys. Similarly, if census data are combined with survey data to generate small area poverty estimates, it is possible that the model has sub-optimal predictive performance due to lack of covariates that are time invariant.

21 This discussion draws heavily from a March 2019 ADB brief titled "Readiness of National Statistical Systems in Asia and the Pacific for Leveraging Big Data to Monitor the SDGs" (Albert et al. 2019).

22 Instead of enhancing granularity, other studies which use satellite imagery focus on predicting poverty or wealth for areas or years where conventional data for poverty estimation are not available. Although the methodological principles discussed in this paper still apply for such research objective, additional investigation may be needed. For instance, it is important to examine whether it is safe to assume that the relationships observed for the years where data are available are stable over time. As this is beyond the scope of this study, the study team encourages future research on this topic.

Figure 13: Maps of Published and Predicted Poverty Rates

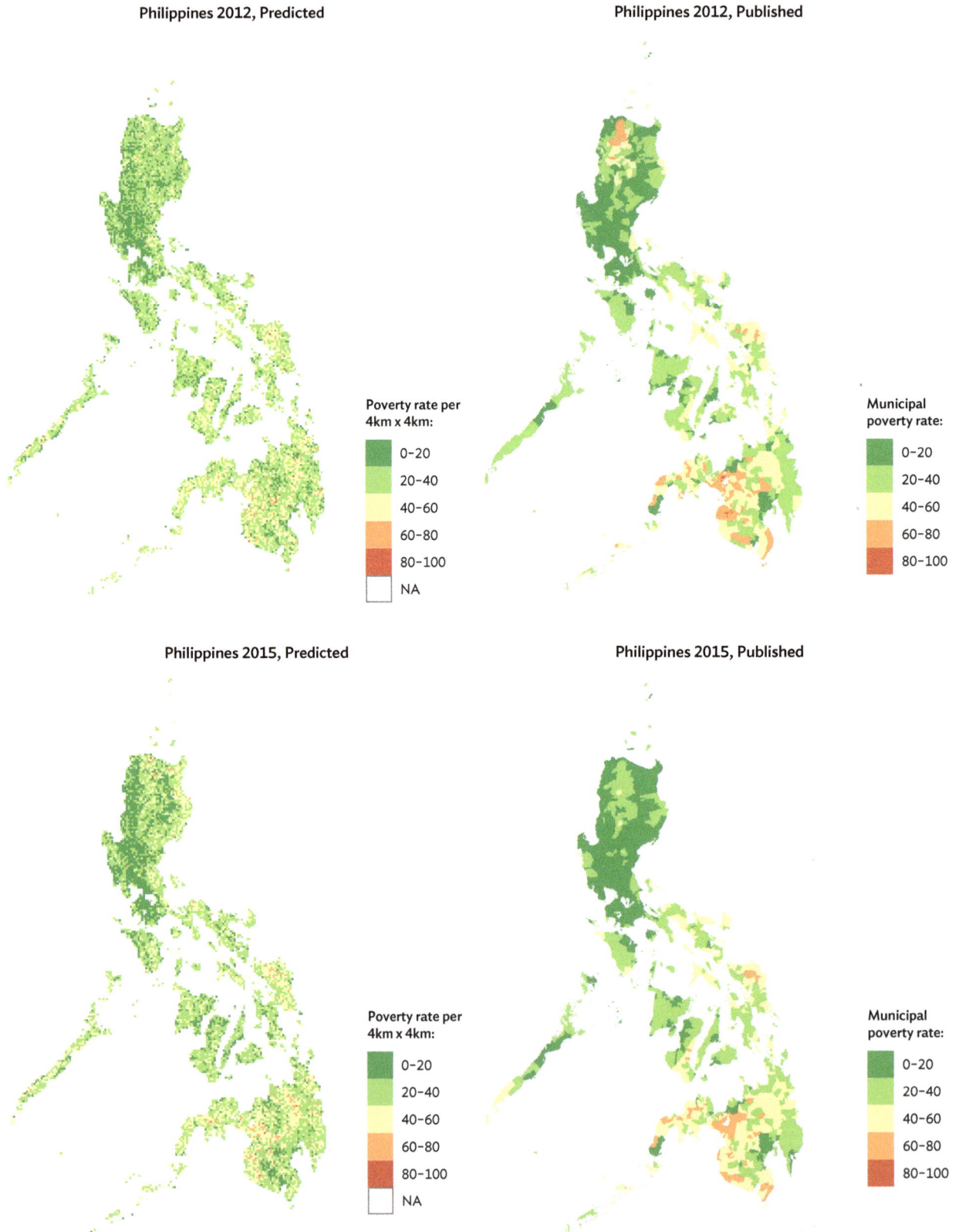

Philippines 2012, Predicted

Philippines 2012, Published

Poverty rate per
4km x 4km:

- 0–20
- 20–40
- 40–60
- 60–80
- 80–100
- NA

Municipal
poverty rate:

- 0–20
- 20–40
- 40–60
- 60–80
- 80–100

Philippines 2015, Predicted

Philippines 2015, Published

Poverty rate per
4km x 4km:

- 0–20
- 20–40
- 40–60
- 60–80
- 80–100
- NA

Municipal
poverty rate:

- 0–20
- 20–40
- 40–60
- 60–80
- 80–100

(continued on next page)

Figure 13: Maps of Published and Predicted Poverty Rates   *(continued)*

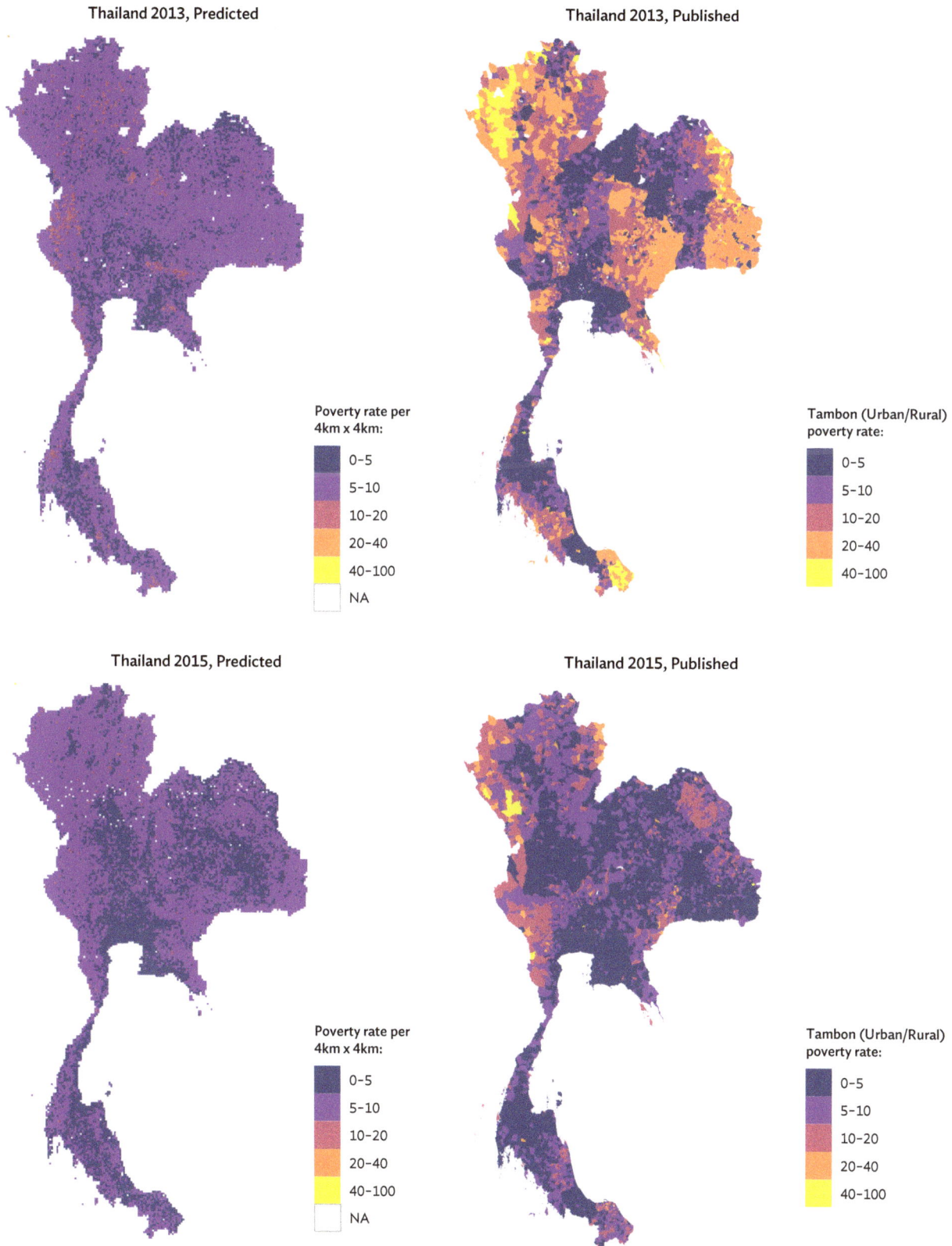

Thailand 2013, Predicted

Thailand 2013, Published

Poverty rate per
4km x 4km:

- 0–5
- 5–10
- 10–20
- 20–40
- 40–100
- NA

Tambon (Urban/Rural)
poverty rate:

- 0–5
- 5–10
- 10–20
- 20–40
- 40–100

Thailand 2015, Predicted

Thailand 2015, Published

Poverty rate per
4km x 4km:

- 0–5
- 5–10
- 10–20
- 20–40
- 40–100
- NA

Tambon (Urban/Rural)
poverty rate:

- 0–5
- 5–10
- 10–20
- 20–40
- 40–100

km = kilometer.
Note: The images present the machine-learning based estimates of poverty rates for every (approximately) 4-kilometer by 4-kilometer grid in the first column, while the second column shows the municipal or city-level and tambon-level poverty rates published by the Philippine Statistics Authority and the National Statistical Office of Thailand. These maps compare the poverty estimates arising from different methodologies. Readers who are interested to understand the factors that drive these poverty numbers could refer to socio-economic reports.
Source: Calculations and graphics generated by the study team.

Figure 14: Calibrated Machine-Learning Poverty Predictions

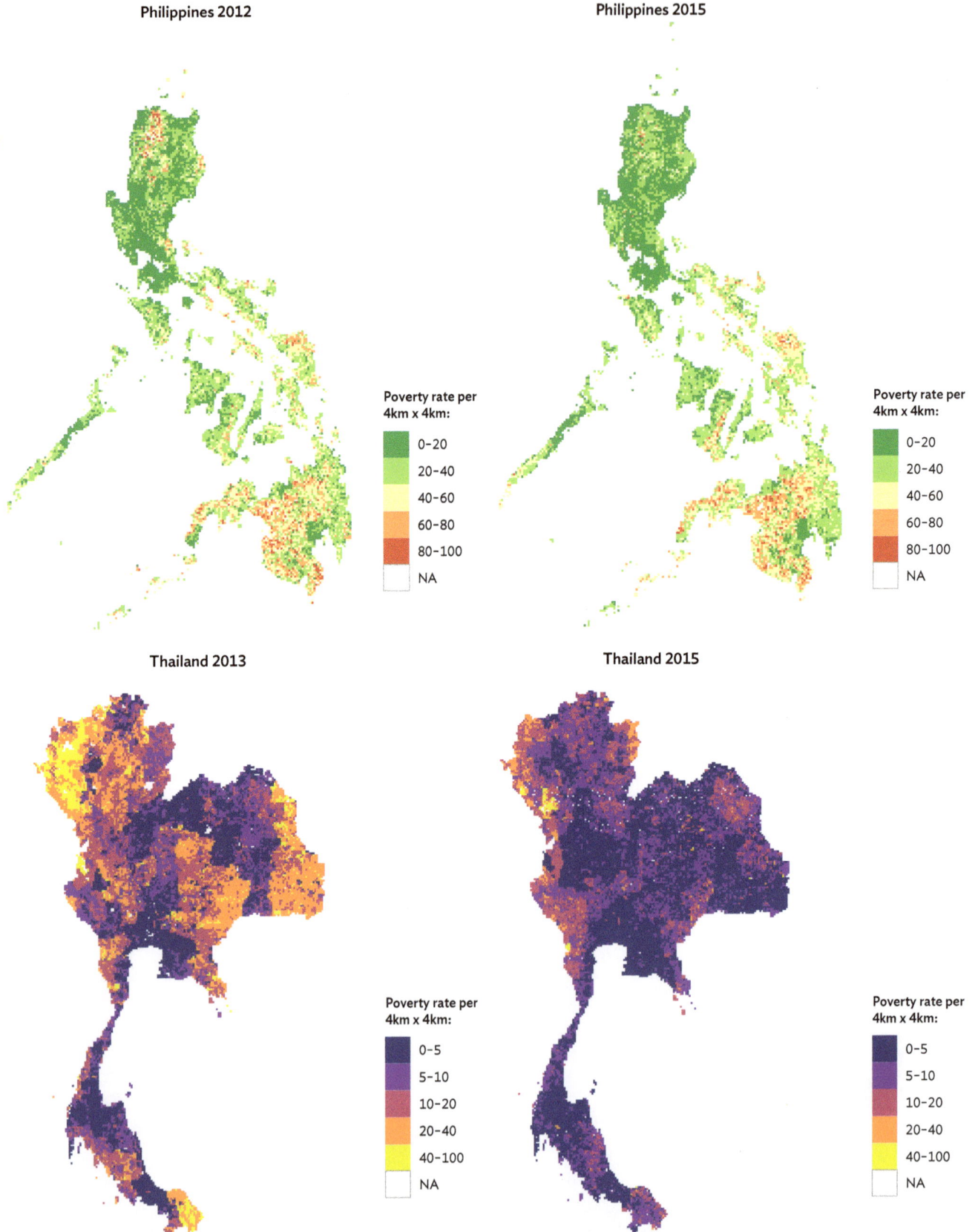

Philippines 2012

Philippines 2015

Poverty rate per
4km x 4km:

0–20
20–40
40–60
60–80
80–100
NA

Thailand 2013

Thailand 2015

Poverty rate per
4km x 4km:

0–5
5–10
10–20
20–40
40–100
NA

km = kilometer.
Note: The images present the calibrated machine-learning based estimates of poverty rates for every (approximately) 4-km by 4-km grid.
Source: Calculations and graphics generated by the study team.

Relying only on traditional data sources risks diminishing the relevance of official statistics. However, if national statistics offices (NSOs) were to integrate satellite imagery and other innovative big data sources into their work programs, they would need to consider several points before they can fully capitalize on these nontraditional data sources.

Access to nontraditional data

In a survey conducted in 2017 by ADB and the United Nations Economic and Social Commission for Asia and the Pacific, 7 out of 16 NSOs in ADB member countries cited access to nontraditional data sources as a stumbling block to incorporating big data into work programs. To access comprehensive digital data on individuals, these NSOs must purchase entire datasets, since those available publicly and for free are scant and may not be statistically representative (Fan and Bifet 2012). Similarly, while there are a number of sources providing free access to satellite imagery (Appendix 2), the resolution of these images is not always optimal for sophisticated feature analysis. Compounding these access problems, many NSOs face the issue of digital traces potentially being incomplete along with the expense associated with securing comprehensive data.

On the other hand, finding sustainable solutions for the issue on data access can significantly benefit the landscape of policymaking. For example, integrating household surveys and census with satellite imagery and mobile phone data provide an invaluable resource for enhanced poverty monitoring (Steele et al. 2017; Pokhriyal and Jacques 2017; Njuguna and McSharry 2017).

Technological requirements

When conducting small-scale exploratory studies into predicting poverty by analyzing satellite imagery, researchers can capitalize on free and/or affordable cloud services that also offer free graphics processing units such as those used in this study (e.g., Google Earth Engine, Google Drive, Google Colab, Jupyter, etc.). However, data sourcing activities on a larger and more meaningful scale might require dedicated servers with high-end graphic cards, bigger and faster hard drives, and local computation equipment.

In general, NSOs are currently using data mining tools that are neither suitable nor efficient for large datasets. To retrieve and examine big data streams, they must upgrade their technological infrastructure and secure the high volumes of internet bandwidth required to manage most big data sources. Improving technological infrastructure in terms of both hardware and software will allow NSOs to download complex data files and to catalog, organize, and process the data in a timely manner. Tools such as Google Colab, Hadoop-MapReduce[23] and cloud computing are increasingly being employed for big data analytics. The cloud is regarded as an ideal computing environment for big data, while cloud computing offers options for accessing and managing large datasets as well as supporting powerful infrastructure elements in a cost-effective way (Agrawal et al. 2011).

To realize the cost and efficiency gains in yielding statistics from big data sources, NSOs must use different types of data processing and analytic tools. These tools can be used for "small data" to extract statistics that are fit for use. They can also help NSOs assess the accuracy of big data to avoid the issues, such as bias, that may be associated with its curation.

---

[23] Google Colaboratory or Colab is a Google Cloud hosted Jupyter notebook service. It offers a free Python development environment which allows developers to write and execute codes through a web browser with an option for free use of graphics and tensor processing unit for enhanced computational capabilites. It is popular tool for Python education, data analysis and machine learning. Hadoop is an open-source software project managed by the Apache Software Foundation and targeted at supporting the execution of data-oriented applications on generic hardware. The Hadoop MapReduce package provides a framework for writing applications that process big data in an efficient manner.

Capabilities

A growing number of NSOs are training existing staff to gain experience in geographic information systems or are employing technical staff who have a background in processing geospatial data. The fact that several NSOs are making investments to expand and develop their skills in geospatial data processing suggests that they recognize the power of nontraditional data sources.

However, the bulk of NSO expertise generally remains in curating data from traditional sources. Most NSOs find themselves without data scientists that have the necessary skill sets to analyze big data. Such skill sets are critical to assessing the methodological accuracy of statistics generated using big data. For example, flu levels in the United States during 2013 almost doubled to 11% from the 6% estimate provided by the Centers for Disease Control and Prevention, which was based on big data on flu-related search terms accessed from Google Flu Trends (Butler 2013). Establishing the reliability of big data hinges on determining whether digital traces can represent information about entire populations.

Credibility is, of course, fundamental to the acceptance of official statistics (Fellegi 1996). The production of official statistics often focuses on precision and accuracy. However, while traditional sources of data yield precise and accurate statistics that estimate parameters of populations, many types of big data do not have clear target populations. Big data sources often come from some other activity, such as making a call on a mobile phone or sharing photos via social media. While it can enlighten, big data can also obscure information, particularly if the analysis involves bias and malice. Besides programming skills, capabilities in handling such issues in big data also need to be developed.

Traditional and innovative data sources must be carefully employed together by NSO staff—from senior management to technical analysts—to produce official statistics. NSOs must also develop the required soft skills to build partnerships in the big data ecosystem.

Data privacy

Data privacy and security are major concerns related to the use of big data sources (UNECE 2013), and satellite imagery is no exception. Resolutions of proprietary satellite images are becoming sharper, revealing more intimate detail in the subject matter, and such images are being taken more frequently. These factors are prompting concerns around potential threats to the privacy and security rights of both governments and individuals (Chun and Atluri 2002).

Mechanisms to protect privacy, such as encryption or anonymization, are not foolproof as it is possible for hackers and other malicious actors to reidentify the sources of the data. Despite the protocols adhered to both by official statisticians and the private sector in relation to data confidentiality, data security remains to be a perennial concern.

Ecosystem

Big data generally exist in a complex ecosystem and are not isolated to particular data sources, sets, or streams (Letouzé 2012). Disruptive digital technologies can empower citizens to collect and use their own data. However, since the rights to such data are generally held by the providers of these technologies, this can have the effect of sidelining producers of official statistics and limiting the influence of individual citizens, private sector enterprises, and other organizations in providing data to NSOs.

On the use of satellite images, the Working Group on Geospatial Information within the Inter-Agency and Expert Group on Sustainable Development Goal Indicators shows that official statisticians recognize the importance of adopting a holistic approach that considers the multiple stakeholders in big data. They must maintain this perspective if they want to capitalize on geospatial data for enhanced development planning and monitoring.

Institutional strengthening

New business models need to be developed to allow NSOs to leverage data resources, human talents, and decision-making capacities. For instance, public-private partnerships can help NSOs promote official statistics as a public good and improve the quality of data. Knowledge materials that discuss statistical best practices and issues to avoid can give countries a head-start on incorporating innovative data into their work programs. NSOs must also familiarize themselves with national and international legal protocols for accessing big data sources and preventing the misuse of such data.

Summary and Conclusion

Globally, innovations in digital technologies have led to a data revolution. At an exponential pace, more and more data are being captured, processed, stored, accessed, analyzed, archived, unarchived, and reanalyzed. The environment for providing statistical data to policymakers and the public has also changed significantly, allowing multiple stakeholders to use a continuous flow of data to make decisions. This raises questions about the prevailing paradigm that underlies the traditional sources of official statistics. This paradigm relies heavily on sample surveys and censuses, which often do not provide statistics that are as granular or as timely as might be ideal to deliver evidence for effective public policies and strategies. In some cases, traditional data sourcing also incorporates the use of administrative records that do not necessarily follow the same standards required for statistics compilation. There is therefore an urgent need for NSOs to reconsider this paradigm.

The challenge to embrace a new paradigm of sourcing data for development is only magnified when the data requirements of the 2030 Sustainable Development Agenda are considered. The data demands presented by the monitoring of the 17 SDGs and their associated targets pose challenges to the resources of national governments. National statistics systems are encouraged to report on over 230 official SDG indicators. The need to disaggregate data—by location, gender, age, and income—for the SDG indicators has made data collection more challenging than ever for these national statistics systems.

There are many cases where national governments are unable to increase the resources allocated to statistics collection and/or development. This lack of resources often requires NSOs to turn to bilateral grants and multidonor trust funds to finance their statistical programs, but such external financing is limited and rarely increases over time (PARIS21 2017). NSOs therefore need to be more creative and innovative in meeting the SDG requirements using their available resources. One area that an increasing number of NSOs are exploring is the opportunity to use nontraditional data sources to enhance the development statistics that are produced from traditional data sources.

Satellite imagery is an example of data source that NSOs do not use conventionally for compiling statistics. This is generally because image data is inherently unstructured, noisy, and hard to process statistically. However, in recent years, advances in machine learning algorithms, particularly in neural networks, have propelled the field of image analysis forward, opening up the opportunity to use computer processing of satellite images to gain statistical information.

In this study, researchers examined the feasibility of using satellite imagery to improve the granularity of government-published poverty statistics. In the Philippines, for instance, poverty (or income) statistics are published at the municipality and/or city level every 3 years, while in Thailand poverty (or income) statistics are published at the tambon level every 2 years.

To enhance the granularity of the available poverty statistics, the study's authors followed a novel approach proposed by researchers from Stanford University and published in the journal *Science*. The first step was to train a convolutional neural network (CNN), an advanced type of machine-learning algorithm that is commonly used for image classification tasks, to predict night light data using daytime satellite images as input. Intensity of lights at night is a good proxy for wealth and human development, and are available at more granular levels, meeting the high volume data requirement for training machine-learning algorithms. In the process of learning to predict night light intensity, the CNN also learned to detect features within the daytime images that can be related to socioeconomic development. The specific information extracted from the images was then averaged to correspond to the level at which the government-published poverty estimates were available.

The results of applying this methodology on specific datasets from the Philippines and Thailand are encouraging. Even using publicly accessible satellite imagery, whose resolutions are not as fine as those in proprietary images, the researchers were able to make predictions that aligned with the government-published poverty estimates. Furthermore, the adopted methodology met the primary objective of providing more granular estimates of poverty in the two countries studied.

Such granularity of poverty statistics is very important because this information serves as important evidence for localized policies and strategies aimed at decreasing socioeconomic disadvantage and social exclusion. Moreover, the recent pandemic brought about by COVID-19 further demonstrates a clear need for high-quality, and more granular data on a variety of health, economic, and personal issues. This vital information

may be more readily available by finding innovative ways to access and analyze big data.

NSOs are exploring various strategies to meet the disaggregated data requirements of development planners and practitioners. The adoption of small area estimation techniques— combining survey, census, and other auxiliary data—is one strategy that more NSOs are following. Other countries are working closely with local government authorities to build their capacity to collect data at the local level. For instance, the Government of the Philippines has passed a new law institutionalizing the country's community-based monitoring system, which generates updated and disaggregated data necessary for comprehensive poverty analysis and other development targets.

Exploring the feasibility of using satellite imagery as an alternative data source for poverty estimation does not aim to replace conventional sources of poverty data: rather, it addresses some of the limitations associated with traditional techniques. Data derived from these new techniques could also be used to validate findings produced using traditional methodologies, thereby building trust in government statistics.

To achieve these objectives, which might also result in significant cost savings, NSOs must make substantial investments in technology and talent. For instance, scaling up from feasibility studies to ongoing and more systematic use of nontraditional data sources requires NSOs to have access to higher resolution satellite imagery and specialist computing resources. More generally, any initiative to integrate big data into national statistical systems will require the forging of partnerships with academic, private, and public institutions to ensure a broad platform for sharing ideas, knowledge, and solutions on how to leverage innovative data sources for the benefit of all.

References

D. Addison, and B. Stewart. 2015. Nighttime Lights Revisited: The Use of Nighttime Lights Data as a Proxy for Economic Variables. World Bank Policy Research Working Paper No. 7496.

D. Agrawal, S. Das and A. E. Abbadi. 2011. Big Data and Cloud Computing: Current State and Future Opportunities. ACM International Conference Proceeding Series. 530-533.

J.R. Albert, et al. 2019. Readiness of National Statistical Systems in Asia and the Pacific for Leveraging Big Data to Monitor the SDGs. ADB Brief No. 106. Manila.

Y. Akiyama. 2012. Analysis of Light Intensity Data by the DMSP-OLS Satellite Image Using Existing Spatial Data for Monitoring Human Activity in Japan. ISPRS Annals of the Photogrammetry, Remote Sensing and Spatial Information Sciences.

S. Alkire, et al. 2019. Changes over time in the global Multidimensional Poverty Index: A ten-country study, OPHI MPI Methodological Note 48. Oxford Poverty and Human Development Initiative, University of Oxford.

S. Amaral, et al. 2006. DMSP/OLS night-time light imagery for urban population estimates in the Brazilian Amazon. *International Journal of Remote Sensing*. 25: 855-870.

Asian Development Bank (ADB). 2016. *Key Indicators for Asia and the Pacific 2016*. Manila.

_____. 2020. *Introduction to Small Area Estimation Techniques – A Practical Guide for National Statistics Offices*. Manila.

J. Blumenstock, et al. 2015. Predicting poverty and wealth from mobile phone metadata. *Science*, 350(6264), pp. 1073-1076.

D. Butler. 2013. When Google got flu wrong. *Nature* 494: 155-156.

C. Castelan, et al. 2019. Making a better poverty map. https://blogs.worldbank.org/opendata/making-better-poverty-map.

X. Chen and W.D. Nordhaus, 2010. The Value of Luminosity Data as a Proxy for Economic Statistics. *NBER Working Paper* 16317. Cambridge MA: National Bureau of Economic Research.

_____. 2011. Using Luminosity Data as a Proxy for Economic Statistics. Proceedings of the National Academy of Sciences 108 (21): 8589-8594.

"Convolutional Neural Networks explained", Youtube video, 8:36, posted by deeplizard on December 9, 2017. https://www.youtube.com/watch?v=YRhxdVk_sIs

S. Chun and V. Atluri. 2002. Chapter 21. Protecting Privacy from Continuous High-Resolution Satellite Surveillance in Data and Application Security: Developments and Directions Edited by Thuraisingham et al. Boston. https://link.springer.com/content/pdf/10.1007/0-306-47008-X_21.pdf

D. Dai, L. Yu, and H. Wei. 2020. Parameters Sharing in Residual Neural Networks. *Neural Processing Letters*, 51, pp. 1393-1410. https://doi.org/10.1007/s11063-019-10143-4

S. Das and R. Chambers. 2015. A Robust ELL Methodology for Poverty Mapping.

Data 2x. 2017. Big Data and the Well-Being of Women and Girls Application of Social Scientific Frontier. https://www.data2x.org/wp-content/uploads/2017/03/Big-Data-and-the-Well-Being-of-Women-and-Girls.pdf.

U. Dorji. 2019. Exploring Night Light as Proxy for Poverty and Income Inequality Approximation in Thailand. 10.1109/TENCON.2019.8929247.

N. Eagle, M. Macy, and R. Claxton. 2010. Network Diversity and Economic Development. *Science*. 328(5891): 1029-1031.

C. Elbers, J.O. Lanjouw, and P. Lanjouw. 2003. Micro-level estimation of poverty and inequality. *Econometrica*, 71(1): 355-364.

R. Engstrom, J. Hersch, and D.L. Newhouse. 2016. Poverty in HD: What Does High Resolution Satellite Imagery Reveal about Economic Welfare?

Exxact Corporation. 2019. *TensorFlow 2.0: Dynamic, Readable, and Highly Extended* [Blog post]. https://blog.exxactcorp.com/tensorflow-2-0-dynamic-readable-and-highly-extended/

W. Fan and A. Bifet. 2012. Mining Big Data: Current status, and forecast to the future. *SIGKDD Explorations*. 14(2), 1-5.

I. Fellegi. 1996. Characteristics of an Effective Statistical System. International Statistical Review / Revue Internationale De Statistique 64 (2): 165-87.

T. Ghosh. et al. 2010. Shedding Light on the Global Distribution of Economic Activity. *The Open Geography Journal* 3: 147-160.

I. Goodfellow, Y. Bengio, and A. Courville. 2016. Deep Learning. MIT Press. London.

A. Hannun. 2017. *PyTorch or TensorFlow?* Github. https://awni.github.io/pytorch-tensorflow/

J. Henderson, A. Storeygard, and D. Weil. 2012. Measuring Economic Growth from Outer Space. *American Economic Review*, 102(2), pp. 994-1028.

M. Hofer. et al. Forthcoming. Applying Artificial Intelligence on Satellite Imagery to Compile Granular Poverty Statistics. Unpublished working paper.

D. Hutchins, et al. 2020. *TensorFlow Fold*. Retrieved January 9, 2020, from https://github.com/tensorflow/fold

Inter-Agency and Expert Group on the Sustainable Development Goal Indicators. 2016. Working Group on Geospatial Information Draft Terms of Reference.

N. Jean, et al. 2016. Combining satellite imagery and machine learning to predict poverty. *Science*, 353(6301): 790-794.

S. Keola, et al. 2015. Monitoring Economic Development from Outer Space: Using Nighttime Light and Land Cover Data to Measure Economic Growth. *World Development*, 66, pp. 322-334.

A. Krizhevsky, et al. 2012. ImageNet Classification with Deep Convolutional Neural Networks. http://www.cs.toronto.edu/~hinton/absps/imagenet.pdf

V. Kurama. (2020, February 24). *PyTorch vs. TensorFlow: Which Framework Is Best for Your Deep Learning Project?* Built In.

E. Letouzé. 2012. Big Data for Development: Opportunities and Challenges (White p). New York: United Nations Global Pulse.

C. P. Lo. 2001. Modelling the Population of China Using DMSP Operational Linescan System Nightime Data. *Photogrammetric Engineering & Remote Sensing* 67: 1037-1047.

S. Marchetti, et al. 2015. Small Area Model-Based Estimators Using Big Data Sources. *Journal of Official Statistics*, 31(2): 263-281.

C. Mellander, et al. 2013. Night-Time Light Data: A Good Proxy Measure for Economic Activity? *Working Paper Series in Economics and Institutions of Innovation* 315, The Royal Institute of Technology, Centre of Excellence for Science and Innovation Studies.

C. Njuguna, and P. McSharry. 2017. Constructing spatiotemporal poverty indices from big data. *Journal of Business Research*, 70, pp. 318-327.

S. Pan and Q. Yang. 2018. A Survey on Transfer Learning. *IEEE Transactions on Knowledge and Data Engineering*, 22(10), pp. 1345-1359. doi: 10.1109/TKDE.2009.191

S. Pandey, et al. 2018. Multi-task deep learning for predicting poverty from satellite images. Thirty Second AAAI Conference on Artificial Intelligence.

Partnership in Statistics for Development in the 21st Century. 2017. *Partner Report on Support to Statistics Press 2017*. Paris.

Philippine Statistics Authority. 2019. 2015 Municipal and City Level Poverty Estimates. Manila.

_____. 2016. 2012 Municipal and City Level Poverty Estimates. Manila.

_____. 2009. 2003 City and Municipality Poverty Estimates. Manila.

_____. 2007. Glossary of Terms. Manila.

_____. 2005. Estimation of Local Poverty in the Philippines. Manila

S. Piagessi, et al. 2019. Predicting City Poverty Using Satellite Imagery. The IEEE Conference on Computer Vision and Pattern Recognition (CVPR) Workshops. 90-96.

R. Pizatella-Haswell. 2018. Fighting Poverty with Big Data: A Conversation with Joshua Blumenstock. Blum Center for Developing Economies.

N. Pokhriyal and D. Jacques. 2017. Combining disparate data sources for improved poverty prediction and mapping. https://www.pnas.org/content/114/46/E9783.short

N. Puttanapong, et al. 2020. Using geospatial data to measure poverty in Thailand (Thai version). Academic Discussion Paper. http://www.econ.tu.ac.th/oldweb/doc/content/1850/Discussion_Paper_No.57.pdf

J. Steele, et al. 2017. Mapping poverty using mobile phone and satellite data. *Journal of the Royal Society Interface*, https://doi.org/10.1098/rsif.2016.0690

F. Stevens, et al. 2015. Disaggregating Census Data for Population Mapping Using Random Forests with Remotely-Sensed and Ancillary Data. PLoS One 10, e0107042.

A. Sumner, et al. 2020. Estimates of the impact of COVID-19 on global poverty. WIDER Working Paper 2020/43. Helsinki.

Sustainable Development Solutions Network. 2015. *Data for Development: A Needs Assessment for SDG Monitoring and Statistical Capacity Development.*

P. Sutton. 1997. Modelling population density with night-time satellite imagery and GIS. *Computers, Environment and Urban Systems.* 21(3/4):227-244.

I. Tingzon, et al. 2019. Mapping Poverty in the Philippines Using Satellite Imagery, and Crowd-Sourced Geospatial Information. *The International Archives of Photogrammetry, Remote Sensing and Spatial Information Sciences,* XLII-4/W19. https://www.researchgate.net/publication/338131416_MAPPING_POVERTY_IN_THE_PHILIPPINES_USING_MACHINE_LEARNING_SATELLITE_IMAGERY_AND_CROWD-SOURCED_GEOSPATIAL_INFORMATION

M.G. Tizon. 2019. Daniel Cabrera, boy in viral FB post, graduates from Cebu grade school. *Rappler.* 16 May.

United Nations. 1995. *Report of the World Summit for Social Development.* Copenhagen.

_____. 2005. *Handbook on Poverty Statistics: Concepts, Methods and Policy Use.* United Nations Statistics Division.

United Nations Economic Commission for Europe (UNECE). 2013. *What does Big data mean for official statistics?* Paper presented at the Conference of European Statisticians 61st plenary session. Geneva. 10-12 June.

United Nations Task Team on Satellite Imagery and Geo-spatial Data. 2017. *Earth Observations for Official Statistics: Satellite Imagery and Geospatial Data Task Team report.* United Nations. https://unstats.un.org/bigdata/taskteams/satellite/UNGWG_Satellite_Task_Team_Report_WhiteCover.pdf

R. Van der Weide. 2017. Poverty Mapping at the World Bank. Manila. https://psa.gov.ph/content/session-2-1-mr-roy-van-der-weide.

C.Y. Park, et al. 2020. An Updated Assessment of the Economic Impact of COVID-19. ADB Brief No. 133. Manila.

World Bank. 2007. *More Than A Pretty Picture: Using Poverty Maps to Design Better Policies and Interventions.* Washington.

Y. Xu, and R. Goodacre. 2018. On Splitting Training and Validation Set: A Comparative Study of Cross-Validation, Bootstrap and Systematic Sampling for Estimating the Generalization Performance of Supervised Learning. *Journal of Analysis and Testing*, 2, pp. 249-262.

K. Yam. 2015. Filipino Boy Who Studied Outside of McDonald's In Viral Photo Gets Scholarship. *Huffpost.* 11 August.

R. Yamashita, et al. 2018. Convolutional neural networks: an overview and application in radiology. *Insights into Imaging*, 9, pp. 611-629. https://doi.org/10.1007/s13244-018-0639-9

Y. Yongling Yao. 2012. Correlation of Human Activities with Population and GDP in Chinese Cities - Based on the Data of DMSP-OLS, *International Journal of Economics and Management Engineering*, 2, pp. 125-128.

Y. Zhou, et al. 2015. Nighttime Light Derived Assessment of Regional Inequality of Socioeconomic Development in China. *Remote Sensing*, 7, pp. 1242-1262. 10.3390/rs70201242.

Appendix 1: A Primer on Deep Learning Concepts

Artificial intelligence, machine learning, and deep learning are terms often used interchangeably, but they do differ in meaning. **Artificial intelligence** is a broad term referring to the creation of machines that are capable of simulating human intelligence in performing particular tasks and solving certain problems. **Machine learning**, meanwhile, is an application or subfield of artificial intelligence. It allows machines to learn progressively from data, without being explicitly programmed to do so.

To better understand the concept of machine learning, think about a child learning how to speak and read. The parent or parents will constantly talk to their child, give him or her books, progressing from simple to complex ones over time. These materials give a child a lot of data to learn from. Similarly, machine learning feeds an algorithm a lot of data and lets it figure things out on its own.

Machine learning is often based on well-established algorithms, which are used to analyze and "learn" from the input data in order to generate insights and inform decisions. Such algorithms usually require complex mathematical calculations to achieve the desired learning patterns. Over time, machine-learning algorithms have become increasingly sophisticated and capable of doing more complicated tasks, up to a point where these algorithms can mimic the structure of the human brain.

This notion of imitating the human brain is the idea behind the use of neural networks (definition below). However, using basic neural networks, some algorithms are unable to progress to tasks that even very young children can tackle with ease. The problem lies in the fact that conventional neural networks generally have only a few hundred neurons, which are connected in a relatively simple manner.

The need to address this limitation paves way for **deep learning**, a subfield of machine learning, which employs deep neural networks, comprising multiple layers of neurons, to perform complex tasks. Consider this image recognition task: If a person is given an image of a number, say a "7", he recognizes it as a "7" even if he has never seen that specific image before. It doesn't matter if the image is colored or black & white, or whether the image is upright or printed sideways. A person can easily recognize a "7" because he or she has instinctively learned the various elements that define a "7", i.e., the number of horizontal and diagonal lines, edges, angles, and so on. Deep-learning models can also perform such tasks because they learn to recognize the characteristic features of a specific object, using deep neural networks via complex feedback loops. In addition to image recognition, deep learning can be used for applications such as speech and character recognition, text classification, language processing, machine translation, social network filtering, and more.

Concepts commonly used in deep-learning methods

Neural network. A neural network is an example of a machine-learning model inspired by the biological neural network that constitutes the human brain. As with other types of machine-learning models, a neural network can learn to perform different tasks without being explicitly programmed to do so.

Structurally, a neural network is composed of numerous nodes and edges. A node can be a variable or a mathematical function connected by edges. These nodes combine together to form different layers within the neural network. The input layer takes in the raw data. In the hidden layers, each node or neuron serves as filter and is activated each time it detects a specific pattern or feature. The output layer simply organizes the identified features into an appropriate category. The best way to represent these connections is through computational graphs as shown in Figure A1.1.

Figure A1.1: Illustration of a Sample Neural Network

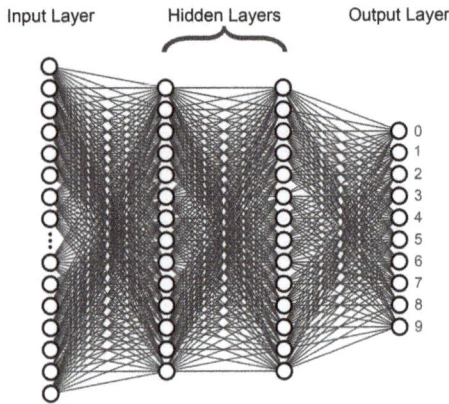

Input Layer   Hidden Layers   Output Layer

0
1
2
3
4
5
6
7
8
9

Source: Graphics generated by the study team.

Figure A1.2: Measuring Cross Entropy Loss against Predicted Probability

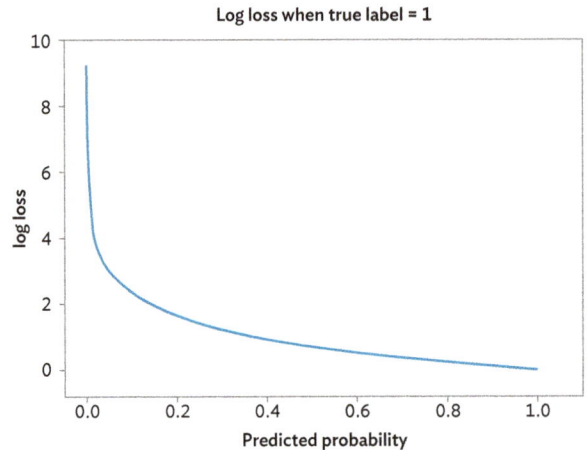

Log loss when true label = 1

(plot: log loss vs Predicted probability)

Source: Calculations and graphics generated by the study team.

Loss function. In machine learning, loss functions serve as a method of evaluating how well algorithms use data to perform the task at hand. If predictions significantly deviate from actual results, loss functions typically yield large values. Hence, algorithms are fine-tuned to minimize the value of the loss function.

There are several types of loss functions, but they can be broadly categorized into two groups: regression-based and classification-based. In regression, the task usually entails predicting an outcome measured on a continuous value scale, e.g., predicting income, consumption, etc. Mean square error and mean absolute error are examples of loss functions commonly used in regression-based tasks. In classification, the task is to predict output from set of finite categorical values, e.g., categorizing images of numerical digits into classes of "0" to "9".

The cross entropy loss function is commonly used in classification-related tasks because it measures the performance of an algorithm whose output is a probability value between 0 and 1. Cross entropy loss functions return higher values as the predicted probability diverges from the actual label as illustrated in Figure A1.2.

Confusion matrix. Preparing a confusion matrix, also known as an error matrix, is another way of measuring the performance of a machine-learning algorithm that has been designed for classification-related tasks. A confusion matrix is a table that maps the frequency of an actual class on each row, and the frequency of a machine-learning predicted class over each column. For example, suppose there are 100 images of the following numeric digits: "7", "8", and "9" (Table A1.1). The far right column shows the number of images of "7", "8", and "9" that need to be classified, while each row represents the number of images classified by the machine-learning algorithm as "7", "8", or "9". Taking the first row as an example, of 50 images of "7", 45 have been correctly classified, one image was mistakenly classified as "8", and four images were mistakenly classified as "9".

Table A1.1: Sample of a Typical Confusion Matrix

		predicted class			# images to be classified
		7	8	9	
actual class	7	45	1	4	50
	8	3	30	2	35
	9	1	2	12	15
	# images classified	49	33	18	100

Source: Hypothetical data generated by the study team.

Optimization. Optimization is the process of enhancing the performance of an algorithm. It entails specifying some kind of loss function and modifying model parameters to minimize the specified loss function.

Epoch. An epoch refers to a complete cycle of presenting the underlying data set to be used for learning. Most machine-learning algorithms need many epochs during the learning phases.

Splitting Training and Validation Set

To assess whether a model has a satisfactory generalization performance, it is important to have a data splitting strategy. In general, data can be split into training and validation sets. Model parameters are estimated from the training set. On the other hand, predictive performance can be gauged through the training and validation sets. Over-fitting occurs when a trained model performs extremely well using the training data set but not on the validation set. If there are multiple models under consideration, the choice usually depends on the model's performance using the validation set.

Concepts used in creating software for deep-learning algorithms

Prototyping. Prototyping is the creation of an incomplete but working version of a computer program. Since deep learning is frequently used to tackle "the three v's" of big data—volume, velocity, and variety—a deep-learning framework that can easily be configured from a prototype is an advantage. Finding solutions to big data problems should not take long. However, given the general velocity of big data, priorities may change in an instant or something may happen far into the project, making significant changes difficult.

Learning curve. A learning curve, also known as training curve, is a tool used to track the training and validation score of an algorithm, for varying sizes of training samples. The curve serves as a useful guide in assessing whether or not an algorithm could benefit from having access to more training data.

Production and scalability. After a deep-learning model has been trained, it enters the production phase. This is the point at which the trained model is integrated with existing software, a website, or mobile application for the use of its clients. Should the resulting research or data be intended for deployment in the future, a deep-learning framework that comes with deployment solutions should be selected. Scalability, meanwhile, refers to the cost-effectiveness and time savings associated with handling large amounts of data at high computational requirements during training or production. Scalability is generally embedded into the hardware and the deep-learning framework. In terms of the deep-learning framework, scalability may come in the form of support for distributed or parallelized training by allocating the model computations to different devices (model parallelism) and dividing the data into packets processed separately by different devices (data parallelism).

Community and resources. Different software frameworks have their own "community" or group of individuals using and contributing to the development of the framework. The bigger the community, the better the support and resources available for its users, including online training courses and references.

At the time of this report, the two most popular and fastest-growing software frameworks for deep-learning were TensorFlow and PyTorch (based on a 6-month study into job listings requiring skills for different frameworks; Google searches; project activities in the software development platform Github; and technical articles published on information-sharing websites such as Medium, ArXiv, and Quora). Both TensorFlow and PyTorch—developed by Google and Facebook, respectively —are open source, deep-learning libraries. The study's authors also considered Keras, developed by Google, which is an application programming interface that runs over TensorFlow, as well as FastAI, another application programming interface that is built on PyTorch (Table A1.2).

Table A1.2: Comparison of Popular Deep-Learning Software Communities		
	TensorFlow	PyTorch
Prototyping	In the latest version 2.0, TensorFlow has adopted eager execution, an imperative programming environment that allows for faster prototyping.	Fast prototyping using imperative programming
Computational graph	Uses static computational graph. However, library called TensorFlow Fold can be used for creating TensorFlow models using dynamic batching to create static graphs that emulate dynamic graphs.	Uses built-in dynamic computational graph.
Learning curve	Coding is less Pythonic thus not so simple for beginners.	Pythonic thus easy to learn.
Production and scalability	Production ready using TensorFlow serving and with easy mobile and embedded devices support using TensorFlow Lite. Features data and model parallelism for ease of scalability. Better for large scale deployments.	Better used in small research and hobby projects. A need for an application programming interface server for production. Simpler distributed training implementation.
Community and resources	A mature framework with a large community, lots of user projects developed, and many tutorials and training modules or resources	A younger framework also with a good community and resources.

Source:Information compiled by the study team, using various sources (Exxact Corporation 2019; Hannun 2017; Hutchins et al. 2020; Kurama 2020).

Appendix 2: Sources of Satellite Imagery

There are three main types of Earth-observing systems, each based on the altitude of their orbit of the planet: low Earth orbiting (LEO), medium Earth orbiting, and geostationary (GEO) satellites.

LEO satellites are typically positioned between 400 kilometers (km) and 800 km above the Earth's surface, orbiting across the Earth's poles. These satellites travel through a fixed orbit at around 28,000 km per hour and can complete their rotation around the planet in about 90 minutes. They have greater coverage toward the poles, rather than around the equator. These satellites are also designed to produce images with greater spatial resolution, taking advantage of their relative closeness to the Earth's surface. LEO satellites capturing images in black & white (or panchromatic scales) can have resolutions as high as 30 centimeters (cm) per pixel, while commercially available imagery with colored or multispectral bands can have resolutions of about 1 meter (m) per pixel.

Examples of LEO sensors producing publicly available images, with well-documented data applications and peer-reviewed literature on sensor applications, include the Moderate Resolution Imaging Spectroradiometer (widely known as MODIS) and Landsat sensors,

MODIS images have spatial resolutions of 250 m, 500 m, and 1000 m per pixel, while Landsat images have spatial resolutions of 30 m. Satellites operated by the European Space Agency, Sentinel 2A and 2B, produce images with spatial resolutions of 10 m to 60 m, depending on the band.

Medium earth orbiting satellites are positioned approximately 20,000 km above the Earth's surface, and have applications for communications, global positioning and geographic navigation, and space environment studies.

GEO satellites are positioned at about 36,000 km above the Earth's surface, so they can remain over the same spot on the planet. The high position enables them to have greater coverage of the Earth's surface, but with an increasingly skewed pixel toward the edge of the sensor coverage. GEO satellites were originally designed for meteorological purposes. An example is the HIMAWRI-8 satellite, which is positioned over Indonesia and can cover half the globe. The images it produces have a spatial resolution of 500 m per pixel, taken at 10-minute intervals.

A typical satellite is equipped with a multitude of sensors for different types of observations. For example, Landsat 8 has the greatest number of spectral bands (11) among the Landsat series. Each of these 11 bands has a specific use as shown in Table A2.1.

Table A2.1: Uses of Landsat 8 Spectral Bands		
Band	**Wavelength**	**Purpose**
Band 1 – coastal aerosol	0.43–0.45	Coastal and aerosol studies.
Band 2 – blue	0.45–0.51	Bathymetric mapping, distinguishing soil from vegetation and deciduous from coniferous vegetation.
Band 3 - green	0.53–0.59	Emphasizes peak vegetation, which is useful for assessing plant vigor. Total suspended matter in water bodies.
Band 4 - red	0.64–0.67	Discriminates vegetation spectral slopes; also measures the primary photosynthetic pigment in plants (terrestrial and aquatic): chlorophyll-a.
Band 5 - Near Infrared	0.85–0.88	Emphasizes biomass content and shorelines.
Band 6 - Short-wave Infrared 1	1.57–1.65	Discriminates moisture content of soil and vegetation; penetrates thin clouds
Band 7 - Short-wave Infrared 2	2.11–2.29	Improved moisture content of soil and vegetation and thin cloud penetration
Band 8 - Panchromatic	0.50–0.68	15-meter resolution, sharper image definition
Band 9 – Cirrus	1.36–1.38	Improved detection of cirrus cloud contamination
Band 10 – Thermal Infrared Sensor 1	10.60–11.19	100-meter resolution, thermal mapping and estimated soil moisture
Band 11 – Thermal Infrared Sensor 2	11.5–12.51	100-meter resolution, Improved thermal mapping and estimated soil moisture

Source: United Nations. 2017. Earth Observations for Official Statistics: Satellite Imagery and Geospatial Data Task Team Report.

www.ingramcontent.com/pod-product-compliance
Lightning Source LLC
Chambersburg PA
CBHW061225270326
41927CB00025B/3498